Will apple pie, Mom, and baseball be replaced by sex, drugs, and acid rock?

American society — especially youth — is in trouble. Dr. John Charles Cooper explains why: "Our age glorifies the antitraditional, the antiestablishment, the antipaternal and the antimoral." It seems as if America is playing right into the hands of the devil, who is undermining traditional, godly values and destroying impressionable youth.

How can we prevent this from happening? In *The Black Mask,* Dr. Cooper alerts parents, pastors, and youth workers to the many devilish devices that Satan employs to entice people. This comprehensive book provides intensive information on all forms of Satanism, from self-styled "dabblers" to cultic and criminal Satanists . . . white witches, black witches, black masses . . . satanic proponents Aleister Crowley and Anton LeVey . . . voodoo, hoodoo, Santeria, brujeria, satanic holidays, and more.

The Black Mask combines the startling facts with balanced, practical guidance. Dr. Cooper shows how you, as part of the Christian community, can witness to and counsel those caught in Satan's web of deceit, so they can be set free through the truth of Jesus Christ.

THE
BLACK
MASK

SATANISM
IN AMERICA
TODAY

JOHN CHARLES COOPER

Power Books

Fleming H. Revell Company
Old Tappan, New Jersey

Scripture quotations contained herein are from the Revised Standard Version of the Bible, copyrighted © 1946, 1952, 1971, by the Division of Christian Education of the National Council of the Churches of Christ in the United States of America, and are used by permission. All rights reserved.

Quotations from "Evil in the Land," by Jeff Lilley, which appeared in *Moody Monthly*, March, 1989, used by permission of the author.

Library of Congress Cataloging-in-Publication Data

Cooper, John Charles.
   The black mask: Satanism in America today/John Charles Cooper.
      p.   cm.
   Includes bibliographical references.
   ISBN 0-8007-5376-3
   1. Satanism—United States. 2. Satanism—Controversial
literature. I. Title.
BF1548.C66   1990
133.4'22'0973—dc20   90-38039
                                                      CIP

Copyright © 1990 by John Charles Cooper
Published by the Fleming H. Revell Company
Old Tappan, New Jersey 07675
Printed in the United States of America

Contents

THE BLACK MASK

1
Satanism Above Ground

The armed guard looked carefully from my driver's-license photo to my face. "I'm here to see the deputy warden," I explained. Still holding my license, the officer phoned the warden's secretary. When he was told that I was expected, he allowed me to pass into the heavily guarded prison.

I now teach college courses at a state correctional institution; I have taught in federal prisons and in state penal institutions elsewhere. When people ask about the difference between students at the highly selective university where I lecture and my prison students, I often reply that the major one is that many prison inmates have tattoos literally covering all their visible skin. SATAN RULES! THE DEVIL HAS ALL THE GOOD MUSIC, and grotesque skulls, knives, anarchy symbols, and horned goat heads decorate the arms of many prisoners.

On that day in late August, 1989, I had traveled to Northpoint Training Center, a medium-security prison near Danville, Kentucky, to consult with the deputy warden for programs. The warden wanted advice on how to respond to several prisoners' demand for ritual objects, occult books, and the freedom to worship the dark lord of evil while incarcerated for their crimes.

All this sounds dramatic, I know, and some may think it creative fiction. Yet for over thirty years I have studied American religious movements—including occultism—using scholarly tools.

When I investigate offbeat or unusual examples of the religious, political, and social impulse, I use the practical application of *phenomenology*. In everyday terms, this means "the pragmatic method of looking and seeing just what belief systems people articulate."

After "fixing" just what is there, I tentatively try to interpret the meaning of belief and behavior. To do this, I use all the resources of the history of religion (that is, religious anthropology), the history of the occult, political and social history, as well as sociology, anthropology, and psychology (especially depth psychology and behaviorism). The eclectic result might be entitled a phenomenology of alternative religious behaviors and beliefs.

I have reported my findings concerning these and other themes in American spirituality in more than thirty-five books.[1] My investigations have included everything from library research to crime-scene consultation. But I abhor sensationalism and have no ideological ax to grind. My goal has been to find the objective truth.

Satanism, in one form or another—as distinct from the multitudinous forms of occultism and "New Age" speculation and magical nonsense—*does* exist in America. It is always the sign of and the result of deviant behavior that often expresses itself in criminality.

Though some have tried to trivialize the threat of the occult to our society, they have merely covered Satanism with a black mask. Behind that facade lie some very real dangers: rebellion against moral absolutes that leads to a disregard for human life, a destructive life-style, and possibly even criminal behavior. I have written this book to point out these dangers.

The Casebook on Criminal Satanism

Consider a few of the recent satanic-crime case histories:

Two teenagers on Long Island, Ricky Kasso, seventeen, and Jimmy Troiano, eighteen, allegedly killed Gary Lauwers, seventeen, a high-school dropout, in a self-styled satanic rite. As early as the seventh grade, Ricky had engaged in digging up graves and writing lists of "the dignitaries in hell." Drugs were a major part of his anti-social life. Most of Ricky's and Jimmy's friends seemed interested in séances and rituals designed to call up the devil. Ominously, over two weeks' time, fifteen to thirty other teenagers were informed of this murder, and some walked to the murder site to see the body. No one told the police until a girl who overheard the murder being discussed phoned the authorities. After their arrest, Ricky and Jimmy were put in separate cells. Ricky hanged himself; Jimmy signed a confession but later retracted it.[2]

In Tampa, Florida, Jonathan Cantero, nineteen, was sentenced to life in prison for stabbing his mother, Patricia Ann, thirty-eight, forty times in the chest, stomach, and back. Jonathan also slit her throat and almost severed her left hand as he recited over her body a prayer in honor of Satan.

Jonathan even made a list of things to do on the morning of October 12, 1988:

> Go to school. . . .
> Visit Mom. . . .
> Stab her dead. . . .
> Sever her hand. . . .
> Recite a poem to Satan.

Like so many self-styled Satanists, or teenagers who invent their own satanic rituals, Jonathan got his information from books on the occult. His murder prayer was taken from one such book:

> Lord Satan, thou knowest I have stricken this woman from the earth, I have slain the womb from which I was born. I have ended her reign of desecration of my mind; she is no longer of me, but only a simple serpent on a lower plane.

Jonathan told police he attempted to remove his mother's left hand to show his allegiance to Satan. He had planned to collect some of her blood in a vial but became frightened and fled.[3]

In January, 1988, a fourteen-year-old boy from Jefferson Township, New Jersey, Tommy Sullivan, murdered his mother and then committed suicide. He was heavily involved in reading occult books and listening to heavy-metal music. Tommy's story sounds like the script of a horror film:

> "To the Greatest Demons of Hell I, Tommy Sullivan, would like to make a solemn exchange with you.

If you give me the most extreme of all magical powers
. . . I will kill many Christian followers who are serious in their beliefs."

Tommy Sullivan was 14 years old when he wrote
those words in his "Book of Shadows," a diary he
kept that chronicled his relationship with Satan.

He continued, "Exactly 20 years from this day I
promise to commit suicide. I will tempt all teenagers
on earth to have sex, have incest, do drugs, and to
worship you. I believe that evil will once again rise
and conquer the love of God."

A short time later, Tommy told friends about his
dream. "He had my face," Tommy said. "He was
carrying a knife and he told me to 'preach Satanism to
other kids, then kill everyone in your family.' "

On January 9, 1988, in the basement of his home in
Jefferson Township, N.J., Tommy murdered his
mother with his Boy Scout knife. He then went upstairs to the living room, arranged several occultic
books in a circle, piled newspapers in the center, and
set them on fire.

Tommy's father woke to the sound of the smoke
alarm and ran down the hallway to find the living
room couch on fire. He extinguished the flames and
shortly after discovered his wife in the basement.

Tommy wasn't found until 9:30 the next morning,
slumped in a blood-soaked snowbank, his wrists
slashed and his throat cut.

When police investigated the murder-suicide, they
discovered that Tommy was involved in Dungeons
and Dragons, a fantasy role-playing game; posters of
his favorite heavy-metal musicians covered his bedroom walls. But police point to his fascination with
Satan as the primary influence to kill.[4]

In October, 1986, an Oklahoma jury convicted Sean Sellers, seventeen, on three counts of murder, for killing his mother, his stepfather, and a convenience-store clerk. Sean, like Tommy, was an avid Dungeons & Dragons player, who wore black robes, kept Anton LaVey's *The Satanic Bible* in his high-school locker, drank his own blood, and in a biology class bit the leg off a live frog.[5]

> In a diary which Sellers called his "book of shadows," he had written, "In the name of Satan, the ruler of earth, and the King of the world, I command the forces of darkness to bestow their infernal power upon me."
>
> Information presented during the trial mentioned such details of satanic doctrines as this "book of shadows," "blood pacts with the devil," "a code of silence," involvement with . . . "inverted pentagrams," "high priests," "recruiters," "heavy metal rock music" and "horror videos." In choosing the death penalty for Sellers, the jury rejected the defense's claim that Sellers deserved mercy because he was a "mixed-up kid" influenced by satanic beliefs.[6]

Now on death row, Sellers has converted to Christianity and attempts to share his story—and a warning—with teenagers, through religious publications.

Richard Ramirez, twenty-nine, the suspected killer of thirteen people in California, named "the Night Stalker" by the press during the terrifying summer of 1985, cut his palm and used his own blood to draw *666* (the mark of the Beast in the Book of Revelation) and a pentagram (an occult symbol) on the floor of his jail cell. When Ramirez was arraigned in October, 1985, he displayed a pentagram drawn in ink on his left hand and shouted, "Hail, Satan!"

In Moscow, Idaho (Satanism is not limited to the great metropolitan areas, but occurs throughout the heartland of America), a reporter interviewed some high-school students who declared themselves to be Satanists:

> Bob, with two earrings dangling from his left ear and rings adorning most of his fingers, spoke openly. His fingernails were filed into blunt points and his clothing, including a long overcoat, was mostly black.
>
> "Basically, an animal sacrifice is totally useless," he said. "An animal is like trying to prime the pump with sand." True Satanists, Bob and the others explained, try to focus energy towards a goal, such as obtaining heaven. There are basically two ways of intensifying such energy: "Through love; sexual intercourse would be the way to say it," said Bob, "and energy that is obtained through the blood sacrifice." Then Bob showed a scar on his arm, which he said was caused by a self-inflicted burn. "This is no call for suicide," Bob said. "And it's not the blood that counts. It's the pain associated with cutting and burning the body that focuses the energy that followers believe is necessary to accomplish a task."
>
> There is no formal name for this group. Mostly young people are involved. "The oldest I know is 22 or so," Bob said.[7]

In Berrien County, Michigan, Captain John Nichols of the sheriff's department reports: " 'We have rumors of people drinking cat's blood, [and] evidence in cemeteries of ritualistic goings on.' Satanism and involvement in the occult is 'fairly widespread' in Berrien County, Captain Nichols observes."[8]

In April, 1989, the Mexican Federal Police, commanded by Juan Benitez Ayala, discovered fifteen bodies on a ranch, Rancho Santa Elena, outside Matamoros, Mexico. The discovery came after a month of searching for an American University of Texas student, Mark Kilroy, who had disappeared in mid-March, during a spring-break drinking spree in Matamoros.

On Sunday, April 9, Serafin Hernandez Garcia, nephew of the marijuana smuggler Elio Hernandez Rivera, was followed to the ranch after he blithely ran a police road-block. Serafin believed he was invisible and immune to police bullets because of the potent magic worked by the smugglers' Cuban-American spiritual leader, Adolfo de Jesus Constanzo.

On April 11, Mark Kilroy's body was exhumed. His death was apparently due to a machete chop to the head. His head had been opened like a hard-boiled egg. The brain had been removed, as had his heart, intestines, and other organs. His legs were chopped off above the knees. A piece of wire protruded from the ground, above his body—or what was left of it. The wire was attached to Mark's backbone, so that when the flesh had decomposed, the group could pull up his spinal column for use in making black-magic necklaces.

An iron caldron, a witch's cooking pot, contained human brains and organs, human bones, a horseshoe, chicken heads and feet, a turtle shell, United States copper pennies, and sticks. This caldron, or *prenda* or *naganga*, is where the sorcerer keeps "secrets." Such a sorcerer is called a *palero* or black-magic priest. Aldolfo de Jesus Constanzo was the smugglers' palero. He killed Mark Kilroy and dismembered the body for "parts" to use in casting spells of protection over the group.

Mark Kilroy was only one victim of Constanzo's black-magic cult at the Matamoros ranch. Fourteen other murdered men were eventually uncovered. Two of these victims had police connections, and several others were rival drug smugglers, so their deaths may have been criminal but not occult. However, one man was said to have been killed because he had insulted Sara Aldrete, Constanzo's female companion (although Constanzo was a homosexual—as were several of the other cultists). That revenge death was ritualistic: The man's nipples were cut off with scissors, and he was boiled alive. Another victim's heart was cut out while he was still alive. At this time, there appears to be no pattern to selection of the victims, but it should be pointed out that Mark Kilroy may have been intentionally chosen for sacrifice because he strongly resembled Constanzo, a reddish-haired Cuban. This substitutionary form of sacrifice is thought to bring greater power to its practitioners.

Constanzo came to the smugglers' attention through Elio's girlfriend, Sara Aldrete, a student at the local Texas Southernmost College. Sara Aldrete was involved with black magic, having read about Santeria, an Afro-Cuban religion that practices animal sacrifice. She also knew Constanzo through mutual friends in Mexico City. She traveled to Mexico with him frequently. Constanzo was "hired" to change Rivera's luck and to insure the drug smugglers' prosperity. Aldrete became a part of the cult, which Constanzo continued to develop among the group, "making it up as he went along," according to one of the members. Constanzo claimed to base his ritual on the re-

cent movie *The Believers*. Close examination of the paraphernalia used and the rituals followed shows a close
similarity to West African black sorcery cults. Constanzo,
Aldrete, and other cult members fled to Mexico City the
day Kilroy was found. When police searched Aldrete's
room, in her Mexican parents' home, they found a blood-
spattered altar.

Three weeks later, Constanzo and Aldrete, along with
the rest of the cult, were surrounded by police in a Mexico City apartment house. Constanzo fired on the police,
then ordered one of his followers, El Duby, to kill him
(Constanzo) and his male lover, Martin Quintana Rod-
riguez. Both died in a burst of automatic fire, and the
five survivors surrendered meekly to the authorities.
Mexican investigators linked Constanzo to the ritual
murder of eight homosexuals, who had been eviscerated
and thrown into a canal prior to the Matamoros killings.

Despite all this evidence—and I could cite many more
cases—some experts among educators, the police, and the
clergy deny that satanic cults exist. The same day, in April,
1989, I received news clippings of the tragedy at Matamoros, Mexico, and a copy of *The Richmond News Leader*
story that declared "Experts Say Tales Are Bunk: Rumors
Abound But Nothing Proves That Cults Exist."[9] What
proof has not been given dozens of times over, for those
who simply open their eyes, look, and see?

The Richmond News Leader article debunks the existence
of criminal Satanism in our society, calling reports of
bloody satanic rituals "urban legend," a false story, un-
wittingly passed on as the truth, like the tales of alligators
in New York sewers.[10] That's marvelously objective and
factual reporting, considering the ritual-murder cases cited

above. The courts that found Jonathan Contero and Sean Sellers guilty of murder in the name of Satan might find such sophistry incredible. One need not propose a "satanic underground" or "Satan's mafia"—ideas that scoffers ridicule—to recognize the widespread phenomena of Satanism's several forms across the American landscape.

It would be good if Satanism did not exist, but it does. We may wish it would just go away while we ignore it, but it will not. If some vague conspiracy theory such as those put forward by Maury Terry or Lauren Stratford were factually correct,[11] it might simplify things, but such theories have no more truth than conspiracy theories surrounding John F. Kennedy's assassination or a supposed communist infiltration of our government.

The plain facts show us that American popular culture spreads Satanism through music, books, films, substance abuse, and the redefined sexual mores of the past quarter century that have legitimized and popularized deviant and immoral behavior. The pop psychology and philosophy called the New Age has permeated every sector of our culture, including the churches, and that Zeitgeist or "spirit of the age" is fundamentally occult, hedonistic, selfish, individualistic, and antisocial. The Satanism above ground, not Satan's underground, should concern us.

2
Shaking America's Foundations

The 1960s experienced a genuine *kairos*, a real turning point in American culture. What I have called *The New Mentality* and Charles A. Reich called *The Greening of America*[1] rose to consciousness among a significant portion of youth in those heady days. Theodore Roszak spoke of the rock concerts, the war protests, the interest in native American and Eastern religions of the late 1960s and early 1970s as *The Making of a Counter Culture*.[2] But all the attempts to understand, glorify, or denigrate the new consciousness and the youth culture it produced came at the end of the 1960s or in the 1970s.

Years before the hippies and the activists exhibited "Consciousness III," a group of younger theologians had thrown down a challenge to traditional Judaism, Islam, and Christianity by declaring "God is dead."[3] The death-of-God movement quickly passed away as a "school," but its influence continued and even grew in the final years of this century. It is not without significance that the Satanists portrayed in *Rosemary's Baby* cried out "God is dead;

Satan lives!" A short and inevitable path leads from the belief in God's demise, as the arbiter of values, to the worship of sensual materialism represented by Satan. In 1967, I introduced the first major study of the death-of-God movement with these words:

> Our survey of the sources of modern radical thought will close with a discussion of the background of *our day's chief theological problem, the question of God,* which we shall identify as *an almost universal sense of the loss of the element of self-transcendence in human life.* We shall see that *this problem is of such serious nature that only the most radical attempts* to recover a sense of the sacred and the experience of self-transcendence *have any chance at all.*[4]

Everyone laughed Thomas J. J. Altizer, William Hamilton, and the other "radical" or "secular" theologians out of court. Indeed, the inchoate, obtuse mysticism of Altizer and the already passé secularism of Hamilton's revival of Ludwig Feuerbach's attempts to identify God with the development of human aspirations and European Philosophy were easy to dismiss.[5] What did not go away so quickly was the real experience of the silence of God; the God-shaped blank in the twentieth-century soul, to which Feuerbach and Friedrich Nietzsche pointed in the nineteenth century, and that engaged the attention of Paul Tillich, Dietrich Bonhoeffer, John A. T. Robinson, Paul Van Buren, Gabriel Vahanian, Martin Buber (who spoke of *The Eclipse of God*), and of the novelists and dramatists Albert Camus, Jean-Paul Sartre, Walker Percy, John Updike, and John Gardner.[6] That is why theologians and religious commentators like Richard L. Rubenstein, Kenneth Hamilton, Langdon Gilkey, and myself kept on investigating the limits of the godlessness of our times[7] and why my 1967 volume was reissued, without amendment, in 1988.[8] Millions of people experienced a hole in the middle of things, and as in physics, theological vacuums pull whatever is out there into themselves. "Out there" was the counterfeit god, the deceiver, in his many forms. The announcement of the death of God began the Age of Aquarius, the era of Lucifer.

From Freedom to License: Man Becomes the Measure

The religious ferment and experimentation of the 1960s did not go away.[9] Rather, the passé spirituality and stubborn rejection of traditional beliefs and values by the "hippies" and the antiwar movement channeled themselves—after Kent State's gunfire—into reactionary new religious movements (promptly labeled *cults*) like the Unification Church (or Moonies) and the International Society for Krishna Consciousness. Other energies pooled in the public subconscious, extending the belief in Hindu reincarnation, Eastern pantheism, and a detachment of "spirituality" from personal and social morality; this would emerge in the 1980s as the New Age movement.

Most Americans, who were never much affected by either hippies or protesters and who found their essential fulfillment in materialistic satisfactions, remained as they were; or fearful of attacks upon a faith they paid lip service to but made little attempt to understand or to carry out in daily life, they turned increasingly, radically conservative.

This turn right eventuated in the mass followings of the televangelists and formed the vague but real substance of the Moral Majority and its evangelical political counterparts.[10]

The death-of-God movement broke like a dynamic summer afternoon thunderstorm, but the hot sun of the general population's indifference to challenges to think about their faith and become spiritually mature came out from behind the passing clouds, and the religious streets of America were dry by sundown.

The wide interest in astrology, mystic visions occurring under the influence of LSD, and séances to raise the dead, witnessed by the end of the 1960s, was more than a passing fad. Widespread enthusiasm for the occult and hallucinogenic drugs of the 1960s and 1970s has continued and grown throughout the 1980s, widening, deepening, and growing to immense proportions. Government statistics say some 42 million Americans have at least experimented with drugs. George Gallup, Jr., and David Poling speak of the flourishing of religious movements and cults outside the mainstream of the established churches. They observe:

> More than twenty-seven million people have been in touch—superficially or deeply—with these religious expressions. For young people under 30, involvement in and exploration of such religious adventures far exceeds the overall national experience. The attention given by young adults is nearly double that given by older adults to yoga, T.M., and the Eastern religions. Clearly the deep spiritual hunger of young people is not being met by the established church.[11]

Other studies of American attitudes and beliefs in religion suggest that many, if not a majority of people, even those with church connections, think of life after death in terms of reincarnation rather than resurrection. The flourishing industries that successfully hawk horoscopes, crystals, and "channeling" (séances) have proved that many Americans see no conflict between church membership and occult practices. Gallup and Poling and many others have concluded that modern organized religion fails to meet the basic spiritual needs of millions.

In 1971, I predicted a revival of mysticism and mystery in the religion of the future,[12] and that has come to pass, to my great consternation. Why? Because such enthusiasm for drugs and the occult is symptomatic of deep anxiety in our people, during this time of radical world transitions. We are experiencing the spiritual parallel to Alvin Toffler's *Future Shock*.[13] Digging into the obtuse nonsense of classical occultism and practicing the mindless rituals of channeling, crystal gazing, casting the I Ching, and summoning the devil indicate a tortured search for personal identity and social meaning.

Such macabre undertakings reveal the zero at the bone of our society, the hole at the center, where the great meaning giver and life director ought to be. Fixation with the occult indicates that our society has neglected the human soul, indeed neglected the human being, in pursuit of the scientific-technological revolution and the power and wealth technocracy has promised and delivered—to some. Occultism, the religion of the Age of Aquarius, the philosophy of the New Age, seeks to escape into unreal fantasy worlds that seem preferable to the real.

Inevitably some people's fantasy worlds will be horror

stories, replete with sacrifices to the dark lord and the demons of the underworld.

The Age of Aquarius Turns Nasty

Occult symbols permeate American life. Zodiac signs decorate all manner of clothing and are formed into all kinds of jewelry for every age group. New Age magazines appear on every newsstand. Channelers, aura readers, gurus, hypnotic regressionists, and parapsychologists turn up on TV, radio, and in the tabloid magazines.

A couple of years ago, I was lecturing on religion in the Age of Aquarius at a small Ohio college. After the talk, we gathered for coffee in the student lounge. My host turned to me and said, "There's a young woman here who has something she wants to tell you." I looked around to see a dark, small girl who was sitting quietly in a loose, yoga-like pose.

She immediately began to speak, in a soft undertone. "I've been on the Tibetan death trip, you know, through all the Buddhist bardos."

I responded, "You mean you descended through all the hells?"

"Yes," she whispered, "all the way to where I was ripped apart."

After a little conversation, I learned that she was now abandoning Buddhist mysticism for "scientific meditation."[14]

In November, 1984, seven college freshmen and sophomore girls crowded into my office at an eastern Pennsylvania university, frightened out of their wits. They reported contact with an "evil ghost." A good deal of skeptical cross-examination proved that this was not a joke; these young people were sincere, even if confused.

On the previous Monday through Wednesday, these young women had gathered around a homemade Ouija board to play a game they called Teacup, a sort of giant Ouija séance. They reported amazement when a "spirit" took control of the cup and began spelling out a story of incest and murder. The more involved the story, the more "information" they received, the more curious and afraid they became. Some of the girls told their friends, and soon a large group of students gathered "to play the game." The "spirit" gave his name—they swore—which they checked at the local courthouse and found belonged to a local family. Eventually, terrorized by the "spirit's" insistence that they visit his unmarked grave, the girls came to me.

I tried to discourage these youth from further involvement in séances, but they were so curious that some of them continued "the game." Finally, all became so frightened that they took my suggestion, dismantled the Ouija setup, and asked the local Catholic priest to bless their dorm and exorcise any evil spirits there.[15]

I could provide an endless list of accounts from a thirty-year ministry on college campuses. Some stories would be amusing, some repellent, others frightening even to the skeptical. Over the last ten years, I have clearly seen the experiences became more brutal, more senseless, more scary.

Criminal satanic activity is not new in America. Charles Manson made a fair approximation of the antichrist when he dreamed of "helter skelter," years ago. Manson's desire to effect Armageddon, the final battle at the end of the age, by ritualistic murder is not far removed from Jesus de Constanzo's ritual slaughter of Mark Kilroy and others in the storage-shed temple outside Matamoros, Mexico. The Beatles' music provided the pretext for Manson's condemnation of Sharon Tate and others to a gruesome death. The movie *The Believers*, made to profit from the popular interest in the occult, provided the pretext, Constanzo is said to have claimed, for his hacking and slashing of twenty-three men; fifteen on the Matamoros ranch and eight in the zona rosa of Mexico City.

Between the 1960s and the late 1980s, America experienced numerous cultic crimes. The mass murders and suicides of hundreds of People's Temple members occurred at the whim of a drug-abusing megalomaniac, the Reverend Jim Jones. The People's Temple leader qualifies also as a type of antichrist. Jones saw himself as a messiah who was not appreciated enough. If he could not have the fame and power he craved, he would destroy those who failed him. The "Son of Sam" killer terrorized the streets of New York with multiple murders. When apprehended, David Berkowitz was identified as a Satanist. In California, San Francisco was besieged by the Zodiac killer, later followed by Richard Ramirez, the Night Stalker, in Los Angeles.

We need not believe in a conspiracy theory to recognize the destructive influence of black occultism upon minds that are inclined toward murder. "When we can no longer believe in God," the great historian of New England Puritanism, Perry Miller, once observed, "it is still possible to believe in the devil."[16]

The Scientific Worldview and a Crisis of Authority

The late twentieth century has perpetuated the myth that people are rational and committed to a "scientific" worldview. However, in any community, in any period, only a small number of people even partially understand the logical scientific outlook. Despite popular perceptions, technicians are not scientists, because they know procedures without comprehending the theories behind them. (Perhaps this is why computers can both make horoscopes and design buildings.)

Fallaciously and irrationally many equate *secular* with *nonreligious*, though secular persons show their religiosity through the appeal of New Age nonsense (which is neither new nor of this age) and the like. Contemporary people are as superstitious as those produced in any century. Reason has not failed nor has linear, logical reason transmuted into some global-village intuition, as Marshall McLuhan claimed in *The Media Is the Message* and *War and Peace in the Global Village*.[17] No, reason and logic have never fully controlled human beings. As Plato recognized in the myth of the charioteer, the controlling principle of the soul must constantly struggle to keep the "black horse" of the passions in line with the "white horse" of reason. The "black horse" seems to have had the upper hand throughout recorded history and has become the runaway favorite in our time.

Rational explanations put forward by scholars, physicians, and scientists convince only those personally committed to a view of life that has intellectual depth. Even for such people, rational explanations cannot begin to

cover irrational fears, deep-seated hostilities, poor inter-
personal relationships, and unconscious prejudices. In
an era that feels the weakness of every form of authority,
from the president to the pope or the all-too-often-absent
father, rational explanations do not answer our most
fearful questions—those about the adequacy of reason
and science itself. Though psychology and sociology as-
sume reasons for the events that befall human beings,
ordinary people often do not. Most of us live in a world
of chance, where, as the inelegant bumper sticker puts
it, STUFF HAPPENS.

Especially in the young, the yearning for mystery in
mankind lingers. Youth search for a breakthrough in the
twilight covering their lives by exploring haunted houses,
playing at witchcraft, reading their horoscopes, and of
late, dabbling in satanic ritual.

Considering the political and academic credibility gap of
the past quarter century, it is not surprising that we have
experienced a serious revival of occultism today. We have
lived through a sustained period of unsettling anxiety,
induced by the rapidity of technological and social changes
and far-reaching political events that stretch back to 1917.
That anxiety, that inner loneliness, expresses itself in
restlessness and experimentation. For example, even in
the face of deadly consequences, thousands risk AIDS
infection, and millions shake hands with death when
they snort cocaine, smoke crack, and inject drugs into their
bloodstreams—all the while expressing hostility toward
every previously respected tradition and authority.

The lonely, questing self that suffers from lack of self-
esteem because it can no more respect itself than it can
respect the self of others, lacks all conscience and has no

sense of honor, no sense of shame. Such people—they are many, and they are in our churches as well as out of them—form no bonds. They marry not for life, but for as long as they feel profit from the relationship, and they "split up" when they feel they can gain nothing more. In the interval between marriage ceremony and desertion, they feel no need for faithfulness to their "partners"; their only loyalty is to their own physical desires.

Such a person sees work not as service to others but as a way to enhance the ego and to provide the material things hedonism demands. Clarity of mind and sobriety are seen as boring, things to escape as often as possible, in altered states of consciousness. Money goes for drugs and alcohol as much or more than for food. This is the first generation to work out for hours in a health club and end the exercise with a bit of cocaine. Nothing matters but sensation and the stroking of empty, deflated egos by flattery, ostentatious dress, the ministrations of hairdressers and psychic healers, "massage therapy," and past-lives regression. These people both inwardly despise themselves and are indifferent to others. In some, the hostility rises to overwhelming levels, and they reach out openly or sneak out secretly, to kill. The most confused and conflict ridden become open Satanists. The black flag of anarchy, grinning skulls, bloody knife blades, 666 logos, and the horned head of Satan adorn their tattooed arms and decorate their black-draped bedrooms. Their haunts are the occult bookstores, where they come to recognize one another and begin to congregate, moving from satanic dabblers to satanic cultists. These are way stations, for the morally sickest, on the way to satanic crime.

Now, perhaps it is clear why the symbol of anarchy

appears as often as the inverted cross and pentagram in satanic graffiti. Satanism is political rebellion, ethical inversion, religious heresy, and suicidal self-loathing, all mingled in one great, taunting gesture of obscenity, thrown in the face of the universe. "Which way I fly is Hell; myself am Hell," could have been spoken by a contemporary Satanist as well as by Lucifer in Milton's *Paradise Lost*. Satanism is the ultimate in deviant behavior, the preeminent in perversion.

3
A Very Brief History of Satanism

If we understand Satanism as the worship of the tempter to sin, the accuser of God's people, and the proud rival of the deity's government of the world, it is difficult to disentangle Satanism from the traditions of witchcraft in Western culture. At its base, Satanism involves a vow of reverence and obedience to the prince of darkness, as demonstrated by the contracts with Satan that surface even today from the occult underground.

Witchcraft is also historically understood as arising from the conclusion of a pact with the devil on the part of men and women at odds with the church and in rebellion against the established order. Consequently, despite the disclaimers of those who claim to be "white" witches, it is not easy to discriminate between witches, especially "black witches," and Satanists. According to *The Encyclopedia of Witchcraft and Demonology*, all the witch-hunters of the Inquisition and later, in Protestant England, saw witchcraft as revolving around a pact with the devil.[1] This recanting of one's baptism and vow to Satan were, in fact, the essence of the "crime" of witchcraft and the basis for any extraordinary powers the witch might possess.

The History of Witchcraft

As early as the time of the church father Origen of Alexandria (A.D. 185–254), charms, bindings, fortune-telling and other occult practices were laid to a witch's *pacta cum daemonibus* ("pact with the demons"). Saint Augustine (A.D. 354–430) saw witchcraft in the same way—and he became the most important voice in Western theology for over a thousand years. Augustine's view of Satan and witchcraft formed the canon laws of the Roman Catholic Church that bore on occult practices. In *Summa Theologica*, Saint Thomas Aquinas followed Augustine and attributed all "superstitions," such as predicting the future, to pacts with Satan.

In the ninth century, stories of people who made contracts with the devil, giving up their souls to him in return for his aid in this life, began to appear. Soon all the details that are familiar to us from contemporary movies and stories such as Stephen Vincent Benet's *The Devil and Daniel Webster* became part of such tales.[2] The Faust legend, based in part upon a historical person, Johannes Faust, who received a bachelor of arts in divinity from Heidelberg University, in A.D. 1509, made the pact with Satan in one's own blood part of Western popular culture for centuries. *Faust*, by the great German writer Johann Wolfgang von Goethe and *Dr. Faustus*, by English dramatist Christopher Marlowe made this man literarily immortal, although the real person was a disreputable astrologer who tried to raise the dead, played cruel practical jokes, and seduced young boys.[3]

The history of Satanism is contiguous with and only occasionally separates from the history of witchcraft. However, these occasional differentiations are very important. For satanic witchcraft is occultism with a pointedly evil, criminal, and antireligious cast. Satanism includes a conscious rejection of and hostile opposition to God, the church, and the established social order.

Clearly much "witchcraft," in a more general sense, was the practice of folk wisdom, centering around medicine, veterinary remedies, and the practices of midwives. On other fronts, what the Middle Ages and Reformation considered witchcraft was really the folk culture of rural women, concerned with love, marriage, sexual attraction, fertility, and childbirth. We must distinguish these *folk witches* from black witchcraft, with its hostile rebelliousness, and those smaller groups of persons more correctly identified as Satanists.

At the trial of Father Urbain Grandier, accused of bewitching the Loudun Nuns, in France, the following pact with Satan was introduced into evidence. It was written backwards in abbreviated Latin:

> My Lord and Master Lucifer, I acknowledge thee as my God and prince, and promise to serve and obey thee as long as I shall live. And I renounce the other God, as well as Jesus Christ, all the saints, the apostolic and Roman Church, all the sacraments, and all the prayers and petitions by which the faithful might intercede for me. And I promise thee that I will do as much evil as I can and that I will draw everyone else

> to evil. I renounce chrism, baptism, all the merits of
> Jesus Christ and his saints. And if I fail to serve and
> adore thee, and if I do not pay thee homage thrice
> every day, I give you my life as thine own. Made this
> year and day.
>
>   Urbain Grandier. Extracted from hell.[4]

We should note that Father Grandier maintained his
innocence, even under terrible tortures. He was burned
alive at the stake, in Loudun, in 1634. Neither the church
nor the state displayed themselves in a noble light during
eras of the persecution of witches.

The hostile, "black" witch can certainly be demarcated
from the folk or healing witches of Western history. These
black witches became *political witches* in many periods but
were especially active in Britain after the Reformation. The
witch laws passed by Henry VIII and Elizabeth I were
aimed specifically at these subversives, who attempted to
predict or cause the death of the ruler as a way of overthrowing the established order. Poison was the preferred
weapon of these criminally inclined occultists, a fear of
which is reflected in the story of Snow White. Black
witches were available for hire, and they used folk medicine in an inside-out, backward—or satanic—way to produce deadly potions that could be put in the ruler's food.
Here murder and antisocial activity combine to define the
political witches as Satanists.

Along with the folk and political witches, another type
of occultist plays a large role in medieval and later Western
history: the *heretical witch*. This describes the person at
odds with the established church, either the Roman Catholic Church, or the established Anglican, Lutheran, or Re-

formed churches in Protestant Western Europe.[5] Both Henry VIII, who considered himself a reformer of the church, and Martin Luther, the theological father of Protestantism, believed sincerely in the reality of witches and of a devil who was active in everyday life. It was the heretic whom the Holy Inquisition of the Catholic Church set out to destroy. It was, possibly, among radical sectarians (today, we would say *cultists*) that the Protestant fathers saw witchcraft at work. By definition, a witch was a heretic, so both the great established churches reasoned that a heretic was a witch, too. Objectively, it is not necessary to think of heretics called witches as Satanists. However, the long, cruel history of the persecution of heretics gave later generations of black witches a severely antichurch outlook. For some, the church seemed to stand for privilege and cruelty to the poor and weak. Perhaps for some of these people who were out of power and out of sorts with the church of their times, Satan seemed a logical alternative as an object of worship. Maybe the folk tales of "Robin Goodfellow," which saw the devil as a "Robin Hood," who opposed the powerful for the sake of the oppressed, stem from the heretical witches.

Aside from the activities of a few perverted, criminal individuals it is doubtful that from the ninth to the eighteenth centuries Satanism as a movement existed. Even witchcraft has a much smaller following than people generally suppose, once we extract from it the folk witches (who were actually healers and midwives). The number of political and heretical witches (who were sometimes one and the same) was always small. These last two categories make up *black witchcraft*, and that is but a name for Satanism.

Modern Satanism Develops

Satanism, in the sense of dedication to the perverse, of hostility against God and government, began in the eighteenth century in the ferment that led up to the French Revolution. It was not a "folk" or common person's activity but arose among the privileged, wealthy classes. Satanism, in the modern sense of that concept, began as a search for sexual "kicks," sensual enjoyment, and power over others. That is what it remains today.

The Black Mass

The black mass, an inversion of the Christian sacrament of the altar, or mass, began in France after the middle of the seventeenth century. Our knowledge of these religious perversions is much sounder than much of the so-called information that has come down to us as speculation or hearsay, since a four-year trial, held at the direction of King Louis XIV, investigated widespread poisonings among the French nobility. Many witnesses testified in the *Chambre Ardente* affair (the "star chamber" or secret-court proceedings), and this evidence has been retained in police files. As a result of this trial, 319 people were arrested and 104 sentenced: 36 put to death; 4 were sent to slavery in the galleys; 34 were banished; and 30 were acquitted. An edict of Louis XIV, in 1682, banned fortune-tellers, controlled the sale of poisons, and declared witchcraft to be an unreal superstition. Louis XIV tried to destroy the records of the trial, but copies escaped destruction.[6]

In the black mass, renegade Catholic priests slashed newborn babies to death over the naked bodies of young women, who served as the altars for these sacrileges. The attenders of these masses were all members of the nobility, several hundred of the highest courtiers of Louis XIV. The "gangs" or infrastructure that made such criminal acts (the murdering of infants) possible were fortune-tellers and abortionists. One occultist-abortionist, La Voisin, was charged with burying the bodies of 2,500 babies. These abortionists were also the local outlets for poisons (usually arsenic) used by married nobility who were involved in love triangles or who wished to speed up their inheritances from aged spouses. Something like a contemporary drug ring existed. Ladies-in-waiting to the king's mistresses were recruited to "push" poisons on the jealous and quarrelsome women who vied daily for the king's favor—and the power that favor gave them. A host of noblewomen and some men (including the captain of the king's guard) were arrested, but no noble person was put to death.[7]

A number of priests were accused of holding black masses, killing infants at some, having sex with the girl used as an altar at others. The Abbé Guibourg (age sixty-six) was said to insert conjurations or prayers to demons in the girl's private parts. These petitions were to two traditional demons of lust:

> Astaroth and Asmodeus, princes of fellowship, I invoke you to accept the oblation of this child for which I ask . . .: That the King and the Dauphin will continue their friendship toward her, that she will be honored by . . . the royal family, that the King will deny nothing she asks of him for her relations or household.[8]

Abbé Guibourg spoke of another mass in which a woman stretched out, her legs and head hanging down from the bed, a napkin with a cross on it over her breast, and a chalice resting on her belly. He cut a child's throat with a knife and drew its blood out and poured it in a chalice. The child's body was kept to make into magic powders. This was done on behalf of a great lady of the court. In some "love" masses, fluids from the woman (at times, menstrual blood) and male sperm were mixed into the blood in the chalice, along with magical powders.

These black masses, or invocations of Satan or his demons, were done not by pagans but by the so-called Christians who were filled with lust for power, with greed for the wealth royal favor could give a family, and with sexual obsessions. Frustrated by the Christian condemnation of the sins of the flesh, these perverted "believers" followed a seventeenth-century "gospel of wealth" in an inverted worship of Satan. In these actions they were aided by clergy who chafed under celibacy and practiced either common-law marriage, who had several mistresses (Abbé Guibourg had three mistresses and many children), or else practiced both homosexual and heterosexual perversions. In their search for royal favor and their lust for fame, position, and power over others, priests and nobility sought the favor of demonic forces.

The church proclaimed Satan was powerless, except for those acts permitted to him by God, but most people (then and now) preferred the heresy of Manichaeism, which saw a good God and an evil Satan evenly matched in a cosmic conflict. Indeed, people found it difficult to believe God was both good and all-powerful, since he "permitted" evil to occur. Therefore, the upwardly mobile felt that if God would not help them in what they were attempting (adultery, fornication, or murder by poison), perhaps Satan would aid them, if they venerated him. The nobility looked for help from renegade priests who befriended the devil.

Many of those who confessed to Satanism later recanted, but the commissioner of police was thorough and careful in detailing the occult equipment (poisons, wax figures for charms and hexes, books on magic and black candles, abortion supplies, love potions, and receipts for large sums of money paid to Abbé Guibourg) discovered at the fortune-tellers' shops. French society accepted the evidence, and a scandal erupted that caused Louis XIV to attempt to suppress the court record. He failed.[9]

Ultimately, the king discovered that his former mistress, Madame de Montespan, was the central figure in this arising of Satanism in France. Like the other nobles involved, she was not tortured or executed. However, the pleasures of the sins of the flesh and the worldly success these noble-women and priests hoped to gain through sex and murder proved incapable of exorcising their anxieties or giving them the wealth they craved. Satan proved to be a deceiver and the occult a maze of useless—and deadly—superstitions. God was not mocked, but many persons suffered horribly.

Ever since, whenever Satanism per se has arisen, it has been an updated yet "faithful" replica of the original outburst of satanic black magic in the Paris of Louis XIV. Ignorance can be overcome with instruction, but moral stupidity continues its devastation year after year. Contemporary Satanism still practices rites that include the elements of the black mass for the same goals and objectives sought by Abbé Guibourg and Madame de Montespan.

Eighteenth-Century Occultism

After the death of despotic King Louis XIV, who declared, "I am the state" and called himself the Sun King or Apollo, the god of cool reason and established order, France became the scene of many Dionysian, frenzied, emotional movements. The Jansenist movement of Port Royal descended from a powerful order stressing God's grace and human sinfulness, but it moved into a miracle-mongering, self-flagellating sect, harassed by Louis XV's police. A revolt against reason took place, ushering in mass hysteria and medieval fears. Even the philosopher Jean-Jacques Rousseau believed in the existence of vampires![10] The so-called Age of Reason was a time of superstition and magnetic attraction to occultists, secret societies, and frauds of every kind. Even Louis XV worked in his own alchemical laboratory.[11] Kurt Seligmann observes:

> There has been no other age in which rose petals, vampires, steam engines, electricity, ghosts, horror and elegance, balloons and garlands, legerdemain and occult sciences, refined ceremonials and hysteria, are mingled so intimately as in the eighteenth century.[12]

We might add that not until the late twentieth century, with its obsession with the occult, under the rubric "the New Age," has a more bizarre era arisen.

In the midst of all this Friedrich Anton Mesmer (1734–1815) appeared. Mesmer was the inventor of "animal magnetism" or hypnosis. Indeed, hypnosis was known as *mesmerism* for many years. Mesmer professed to be able to cure diseases by the use of rays (the aura) that emanate from the body. One thinks of the "healing touch" and various massage practices even of trained nurses in our own day. Stupidity never ends.

The seventeenth century also saw the rise of secret societies, the Masonic Lodge and Rosicrucian Society being the most important and enduring. They emphasized the esoteric, the supposed reclamation of ancient traditions, and the joy of involved ritualism.

Finally, occult personalities of the first order, such as the Count of Saint Germain and the magician and antimonarchist Cagliostro, who founded an Egyptian rite or lodge, were the object of many tales and rumors through this period. The guillotine of the French Revolution removed many noble occultists, but magic and the attraction of the forbidden rites remained.

Remember, in historical witchcraft the black mass began late in the seventeenth century. Wanting to guarantee good futures for themselves, and full of the thrill of hidden blasphemy and sexual indulgence, Louis XIV's nobles—chiefly women—hired fifty or sixty renegade Catholic priests to conduct these "special" masses, based on the earlier (and orthodox) masses of intention, in which a believer petitioned God for a special favor.

The black mass was purely an invention of this period. The *Malleus Maleficarum* (or *The Witch Hammer*) of 1486, which was produced by Roman Catholic theologians and canon lawyers for use in the Inquisition, knows nothing of a black mass.[13] The priests who devised the mass for Satan had two earlier heretical rites to use as guides. The church had condemned a mass of the dead, which was used by wicked persons, not to memoralize a deceased one. Later, perhaps after the rise of the movement of courtly or romantic love (in the late fourteenth century), an amatory mass ("mass of love") was devised by heretical priests, in order to help a lover win the hand of a desired partner. Indeed, the priests who created the black mass by reversing everything in the Catholic mass also performed amatory masses for the noble women who were their chief clients. These aristocratic hangers-on at the French court wanted the king to choose them as his mistresses—and were willing to ask the demons for help in realizing their desires. This, despite many unfounded claims of a long tradition of devil worship, is the historical origin of satanic worship.

The black mass as it is popularly thought of was a *literary* creation that appeared in such works as *Justine*, by the infamous Marquis de Sade. Not until over a hundred years later, when witchcraft as a folk practice had ceased to exist, did certain romantics with a perverted view of religion, morality, and society invent the black mass known to us through books and films: a service dedicated to the antichrist and untruthfully claimed to be a remnant of ancient practices. Joris-Karl Huysmans presents such a picture in his book, *La Bas*.[14]

Nineteenth-Century Occultism

Romanticism's Reaction to Rationalism. The 1800s opened with rationalism triumphant in the Western world.

The deists still influenced the religious life of Britain and the newly independent United States. In France, the Revolution exalted "the goddess Reason" over the discredited Catholic Church. God, according to the rationalists who remained deists, was the grand, high architect of the universe, the cosmological watchmaker, whose existence could be proved by the "argument from design." By that, William Paley and others meant that the design of the human eye and of many intricate elements in man and nature demonstrated their design and creation by an intelligent planner. Other rationalists, however, like Thomas Paine, in America, and many in France, became atheists. For both simple and sophisticated believers, neither rationalist view satisfied. As the Jansenist mathematician-philosopher Blaise Pascal put it: "The God of Abraham, the God of Isaac, the God of Jacob, the Father of our Lord Jesus Christ, and not the god of the philosophers."[15]

Jansenism was a reactionary movement within Catholicism, which sought to recover the theology of Saint Augustine and had many similarities to the thought of Martin Luther and John Calvin. It quickly became more opposed to prevailing attitudes, stressing miraculous healings and other miracles. The Jansenists stressed faith in the supernaturalism of God, Christ, and the Christian mysteries. Pure reason was not enough to feed the soul. In Denmark, Søren Kierkegaard held this position.

Later in the 1800s, Romanticism of a more secular sort developed, stressing the human emotions, particularly the erotic feelings and the delicious thrills of fear engendered by horror stories. The intellectual journey of these literary romantics was often prompted by their desire to escape rationalistic moral self-discipline in order to lose themselves in promiscuity and, for some, in substance abuse. Mary Wollstonecraft Shelley wrote *Frankenstein*. Bram Stoker produced *Dracula*. The horror literary genre was born—a genre much developed and exploited in the films of the twentieth century. Samuel Taylor Coleridge wrote "Kubla Khan," a poem produced in a euphoria brought on by opium. The foundations of a subculture fascinated by the dark forces of evil and by self-destruction were laid down almost a century and a half ago.

Under what many felt was the repression of Victorian manners and mores, even sillier forms of romanticism developed, particularly in Britain. These involved the rise of the Gothic novel and the attempt to rehabilitate witchcraft. These fictional attempts to show an unbroken line of witches from the pre-Christian past up to the present went on into the 1940s. Gerald Gardiner proposed that witches were practitioners of the "old religion" of the Celts. Margaret Murray claimed witchcraft was ancient and beneficial. Both made room for feminine religious leadership and attempted to make the occult more respectable and less mysterious. The "evidence" both claimed was undoubtedly false.

Satan, in the form of the devil, or the horned god of witches, made his reappearance in these supposedly rehabilitated forms of "wicca" or witchcraft. The horned god, or the disguised high priest (or *warlock*) of the witchcraft coven symbolized the fertility god, whose role was to interact with the high priestess, the symbol of the fecund earth (or mother earth). The "sacrifices" to the god—or goddess—of the witches were sky-clad (naked) dancing and sexual performances (to encourage fertility). These nineteenth- and twentieth-century romantics were not sadomasochistic. As yet no hard-core, cruel, blood sacrifices to Satan had developed. The cruel and insane aspects of the occult were practiced by the antiestablishment, substance abusing upper-class, male members of the Hell-Fire Club, in Britain. There seems to be no connection between the Hell-Fire Club and witchcraft. Yet these two developments pointed toward a sadder future in the late twentieth century.

Contemporary deviant or destructive occultism originated in the romantic movements of the late nineteenth century. The continuing stream of superstition in the Age of Reason and the pragmatism of an age of expansion and conflict in the nineteenth century was deepened by the romanticizing of magic and witchcraft by Éliphas Lévi (1810–1875), of France. He popularized occultism in Europe, and through Aleister Crowley, in America. Lévi stressed magic as a means to power and emphasized sex and drug abuse. In the 1840s a movement began that resulted in "the Church of Carmel," led by a defrocked priest and an ex-nun. Reportedly this group ritually sacrificed a baby born to Bonllan and Adele, the leaders, on January 8, 1860. If the report is factual, this would be the first documented human sacrifice in destructive occultism. The use of drugs (cocaine, hashish, and morphine) attracted the Marquis de Guaita (1861–1897). He and others founded the Kabalistic Society of the Rosy Cross in 1888, and satanic worship soon dominated the group.

Other Nineteenth-Century Influences. The nineteenth century was far more like the twentieth century than most people either know or acknowledge. Both religious and secular (socialist) Utopian sects multiplied. Communalism flourished among radical dissenters like the Amish, the Brethren, the millennialist Shakers and the free-loving Oneida Community. Poets—and the fictional detective Sherlock Holmes—sought to open doors of their perception with drugs. The horror of American Civil War battlefield surgery without anesthesia produced a generation of opium addicts. Alcohol was consumed in destructive amounts in the cities of Britain and America and on the raw frontier.

The West also became fascinated by reports of the strange beliefs of the peoples brought into the far-flung European empires or met by the sailors of the American China clippers. Transcendentalism in philosophy, Unitarian theology, and a new, rich American literature made the ideas of reincarnation, karma, and pantheistic spiritualism popular. The 1960s invented nothing essentially new, nor is the New Age of the 1980s at all novel. The ideas (and misconceptions) that fuel the wide interest in the occult today all first became part of the Western consciousness in the nineteenth century. Vaguely Eastern ideas played a major role in European and American intellectual life, as the rise of New England's transcendentalism and the development, a century later, of Jungian "psychology" attest. Interestingly, religious persons, clergy, and seminarians welcomed Jungian thought. Indeed, M. Scott Peck, a contemporary psychologist, is a favorite of the clergy and church members, though his "system" turns out to be an occult version of Hinduism.[16] Sigmund Freud may have been a materialist, but he was right when he expressed horror at Jung's dabbling in the occult. Freud feared that the occult, like a "tide of mud," would overwhelm science. His fears, as far as much psychology and popular culture are concerned, have been realized.

Twentieth-Century Satanism

Aleister Crowley. At the beginning of this century, a most important figure in black magic, the witchcraft of Satanism, appeared. He was Aleister Crowley (1875–1947), a drug abuser and sexual pervert who was fascinated by ceremonial magic. Crowley carried the drug use and sex magic of earlier occultists to its uttermost in the OTO, or the *Ordo Templi Orientis*, a German secret sexual magic group.

Two of Crowley's most important works are *777* and *The Book of the Law*.[17] As its primary object, *777* had the construction of a magical alphabet that would synchronize and synthesize the occult "wisdom" of all Eastern and Western traditions. In Egypt, where he researched mysticism, Crowley wrote *The Book of the Law*,[18] stressing the supremacy of the will:

> "There is no god but man."[19]
> "Man has the right to live by his own law."[20]
> "Do what thou wilt shall be the whole of the law."[21]

Crowley had received what he felt was a revelation from the ancient gods of Egypt, and he glorified the perfection and hardening of the human will as the major element in "magik" [*sic*]. Crowley believed that the discovery of true willpower was the "Great Work" that made one a master magician, or magi. This willpower could come only through the destruction of what is ordinarily considered the self and the mind's discrimination between good and evil, one's existence and that of the world.

Around 1920 he founded the *Abbey of Thelema* ("Abbey of Will") in Sicily, where the most debased pansexual orgies were held under the influence of great doses of hashish, opium, and cocaine. Crowley, a sex-obsessed bisexual, encouraged a "celestial hierogamy" ("a heavenly sacred marriage") to raise the power of the will of a group of disciples, under their master, to work "sexual magic." He urged his followers to gash their arms with razors every time they inadvertently said, "I." These orgies and related drug abuses put several of Crowley's concubines (as he called them) into the hospital and caused the death of a child, under circumstances never explained. After this, the abbey was dissolved. While Crowley may be called a Satanist only in the moral sense that he rejected the concept of God taught in all great religions and embraced the contrapuntal tradition of the dark, the self-willed, and the sensual, he has been used as the bridge between the black-mass originators of the late seventeenth century and Satanists in America today.

Crowley spent years in California, and numerous occult groups there trace their foundation back to him. He profoundly influenced Anton LaVey and contemporary Satanism.

Anton LaVey. Anton Szandor LaVey, a man of clouded background, ran away from home at the age of seventeen to work in a circus. He later became a carnival hypnotist and then an organ player for a carnival strip show. On Sunday he says he saw the same men at the evangelist's tent, where he played the organ, as he had seen at the strip shows the previous evening. Later, he became a crime-scene photographer for the San Francisco police department. His experiences on the rough fringes of life convinced him that most people are hypocrites.

LaVey is the best-known religious Satanist. With his shaved head, goatee, and black coat and hat, he was the cover story for the *Washington Post Magazine* as recently as February, 1986. Stories about the nude women sprawled atop his satanic altar at his San Francisco church have been reported by the press.

Almost single-handedly, LaVey literally created contemporary Satanism. The basis of that creation is his founding of the Church of Satan, in California, and the 1969 publication of *The Satanic Bible* (which has sold more than 500,000 copies).[22] He brought about both events on Walpurgisnacht, the most important festival in witchcraft and magic. LaVey declares:

> A glow of new light is borne out of the night (of the Twilight of God; the Death of God) and Lucifer is risen, once more to proclaim: "This is the age of Satan! Satan rules the Earth!" The gods of the unjust are dead. This is the morning of magic, and undefiled wisdom. The FLESH prevaileth and a great Church shall be builded, consecrated in its name. No longer shall man's salvation be dependent on his self-denial.[23]

His introduction concludes with:

> Regie Satanas! [Satan Rules!]
> Ave Satanas!
> Hail Satan![24]

Those who saw the film *Rosemary's Baby* will recall that these are the words proclaimed by the satanic coven at the birth of Rosemary's dreadful child, the son of Satan. LaVey was the consultant on the occult for that movie.

Satanism has been good for LaVey, since he shaved his head, announced God was dead, and formed the Church of Satan on April 30, 1966. He collects classic cars and has several luxurious homes and a 185-foot yacht at his disposal. He charges $100 a session for satanic counseling and receives royalties from several books.

This twentieth-century Satanist remains something of a carnival huckster. For him, "Satan is a symbol, nothing more." He says he believes in neither God nor Satan. He sees Satan as a symbol of the carnal nature, with its lust, greed, vengeance, and ego drives that LaVey says Christianity has labeled "evil." He rejects the supernatural, an afterlife, heaven, and hell. There is no sin. Man is a superior animal and should worship his own ego.

In 1972 LaVey published (as a mass-market paperback) *The Satanic Rituals*.[25] The foreword claims:

> . . . We are experiencing one of those unique periods in history when the villain consistently becomes heroic. The cult of the anti-hero has exalted the rebel and the malefactor.
>
> Because man does little in moderation, selective acceptance of new and revolutionary themes is nonexistent. Consequently all is chaos, and anything goes, however irrational, that is against established policy. Causes are a dime a dozen. Rebellion for rebellion's sake often takes precedent over genuine need for change. *The opposite has become desirable, hence this becomes the Age of Satan.*

Dire as this appears, yet when the dust of the bat-
tles settles what truly needed changing will have been
changed. The sacrifices will have been offered, human and otherwise, so that long-range development
might continue, and stability return. Such is the od-
yssey of the Twentieth Century.[26]

This is an astute observation. It is certainly not wrong to
acknowledge LaVey's insight here, since good religionists
must "tell the truth and shame the devil"! Our age glorifies the antitraditional, the antiestablishment, the antipaternal, and the antimoral. LaVey remembers what all too
many so-called Christians forget: The *anti*, the "other," is
Satan: "The Child has emerged in the form of Satan—the
opposite."[27]

Here, then, is recognition, from the satanic side, that
the real influence of contemporary antisocial and criminal
events is the spirit of the age in which we live: what I
called "the contrapuntal tradition" in my book *The New
Mentality*—the fountainhead of "the new morality," feminism in its extreme form, "gay" liberation and the sanc-
tioning of abortion, the "nontraditional family," and the
recrudescence of occultism in dozens of "new religions"
and the New Age. Popular culture, the way we see ourselves and the way we are with one another, is the source
of satanic activity, not some "organized conspiracy." Pogo
put it well: "We have met the enemy, and they is us." We
are the people our parents warned us against. We, who
call *license* "freedom," are the sources from which the
young and the unbalanced draw the elements to create
their individual "hells."

The Rise of Spiritual Anarchy. The black flag traditionally symbolizes anarchy, the philosophy of unbridled individualism and antiestablishmentarianism. In Spain, anarchists fought in the Spanish Civil War of the 1930s. In the early years of this century, anarchists assassinated a number of national leaders, including an American president, William McKinley. In the twentieth century, destructive occultism, of which Satanism is the most extreme expression, functions as spiritual anarchism. It is utter selfishness, pure egotism in action, and a quest for personal power and unlimited sensual pleasure. Destructive occultism represents the triumph of the will and the rejection of all authority, with the exception of the authority of those spirits (demons) who stand against God, government, and all authority.

Much destructive occultism (or deviant occultism) in the contemporary world has a radical feminist basis. The attack on God the Father and on the traditional Christian church, including the traditional concept of the family, has not developed as a response to the undoubted male chauvinism of much of American, European, Asian, and African history, but seeks to reject all limits to self-indulgence. Mary Daly's attack on Catholicism passed the limits of criticism (as seen in other Catholic thinkers like Rosemary Ruether) and became pathological.[28] The aptly named "witches from hell" kind of radical feminism is occult in the most destructive sense. This movement is aggressively homosexual (lesbian), antimale, and antisocial.

Other deviant occultic groups grow out of an exaggerated masculine chauvinism, a sadomasochistic masculinity of chains, leather, and bravado. This includes the Hell's Angels type of satanic involvement. Of course, not all or even most Hell's Angels practice Satanism, but some do. The psychopathology of some bikers' personalities precisely parallels that of the Satanist: an insecure person who demands total control, has poor peer-relations skills, an inability to accept authority, and a fascination with weapons and violence, and an addictive relationship to drugs. Such people could become part of either group.

Satan and the Church

As a result of the oppression of serfs that was part of the feudal system, in the Middle Ages Satan may have gotten a "good" name among the lower classes, because the church supported—and was—the establishment.

During the Reformation, Luther, perhaps the last important medieval figure and the first important modern thinker, remained medieval in his literal, mythic religious outlook. While William Blake may have seen the Virgin Mary in a tree, and simple peasant children saw saints and miracles, Luther saw the devil in his tower study—and threw something obscene at him (usually euphemistically called "an inkwell"). Luther spoke of Satan in terms of magical realism, and that literalism took hold of the popular Protestant imagination in the same way that the realism of Catholic miracles and visions retained their hold on populations for centuries.

The development of the apocalyptic millennial outlook, which saw the history of the universe as the struggle between the kingdom of God and the kingdom of Satan, perpetuated the importance of Satan in the popular imagination. In all events, those who stood foursquare for the Christian faith and those who opposed it together invented the madness of occultism and together reinfected each other in each succeeding century.

As one baptismal formula has it: "Do you renounce the devil, and all his works, and all his ways?" The response to which is: "Yes, I renounce them."[29]

The orthodox Christian doctrine of the relationship of Satan to mankind since the victory of the cross does not glorify the enemy. Early church fathers, notably Irenaeus of Lyons, proposed the *Christus Victor* ("Christ, the Victor") concept of the atonement, stressing Christ's defeat of Satan. Irenaeus simply pulled together the main lines of Paul's atonement argument in the Epistle to the Romans, where Paul hammers home Christ's work on the cross as the conqueror of sin, death, the devil, and the power of the Law to accuse the Christian conscience.

Martin Luther clearly identified all these dramatic powers as the sinner's experience of the wrath of God. In God's plan of salvation, God's wrath, his "left hand," drives man to repentance and faith in Christ. Luther, who took the existence of the devil very seriously, nonetheless saw Satan as only a creature, used against his will as part of the Omnipotent God's plan of salvation.

Most notably, the Roman Catholic Church has kept alive the fact that Satan *is*, without glorifying him in the manner of much sectarian Protestant preaching. The emptiness and hollowness of Satan's power and the self-destructiveness of engaging in sin need to be stressed. But above all, the reality of temptation and the need to truly *renounce* the agent of temptation needs more stress in all churches. To renounce is to put behind one, to give up, to trample underfoot the black flag of spiritual revolt.

Perhaps all communions should join the liturgical

churches in insisting on the renunciation of the devil at baptism. Perhaps, too, all churches should deal thoroughly with religious cults and occultism in their confirmation or membership classes. Even more, the churches should pay more attention to the alienated, confused, and susceptible young people everywhere around us, who are as "lost" as any heathen in the jungles far away.

Such attention to Christian duties might well be joined to a decent moratorium on pronouncements by preachers and self-styled "experts" on Satanism who, in the long and short run, do more harm than good. *Renounce* means just that. To put the great liar behind us includes refusing to reempower his broken weapons of deceit. Instead, the church might preach Christ as the Victor, not only over the objective powers of evil but also over the subjective ones; the dark, inward doubts and appetites that work within every person. Salvation, the antithesis of demonic possession, ought once more to be framed in the words of Martin Luther: that Christians are *simel iustus et peccator*- "simultaneously saved *and* sinners." We are never in a spiritual state that does not require daily repentance of sinfulness. We never reach a place where we can stop renouncing the devil and all his works. The church is a place for sinners to be welcomed. God *must* love them; his Son *died* for them.

In the 1990s our attitude toward Satan must become same as Paul's in the first century: He is beaten when come to faith.

4
Modern Satanism's Many Faces

Satanism in America is not one movement, but many relatively independent movements, arising out of the occult-laden, valueless popular culture of the streets, sexual customs, broken homes, movies, television, books, magazines, bookstores, and mail-order advertisements. More than any other form of human endeavor, Satanism is a do-it-yourself religion that puts one in mind of the old expression: "as ugly as homemade sin."

Dabblers

People, especially junior-high and high-school youths, read about Satanism and the occult and build up groups and rituals out of bits and pieces of their reading and movie viewing. This self-initiated form is known as dabbling. *Dabblers* may never go beyond reading about rituals, or they may combine with others into small groups. They may never do anything overtly antisocial and parents or teachers may not recognize them as dabblers, or they may degenerate into drugs and promiscuity; some may even be drawn into murder. The loose circle of high-school students on Long Island, discussed in chapter 1, was a group of dabblers who moved all the way to criminal Satanism, without intermediate stops. Solo dabblers, too, may descend into madness, like the boys in New Jersey and Florida, or Sean Sellers, in Oklahoma.

A dabbler may become more genuinely interested in the occult, even to the point of obsession. Such a deeply interested person will generally make contact with others of similar interests. Here the teenage circle, or coven, may develop.

Dabblers are also known as *self-styled Satanists*. Teenagers imitate the books they read; the movies they see; and the "thrash metal" rock groups (a subcategory of "heavy metal" music) they admire. They may or may not "believe" in Satan, but their lives are full of drug abuse and, often, of senseless violence.

Some such Satanists are rebelling against normative religion—and most of these are reacting to a strict, fundamentalist upbringing—but more often such young people have had little or no structure, be it religious or familial.

Magic and fantasy fascinate these young people, but this age group also includes much emotional turmoil. Adolescence is an opportunity to rebel against conventional authority, to discover a sense of belonging, and to experience empowerment. Unfortunately, young people tend to take a phrase like, "If it feels good, do it," much more literally than adults. Satanism blesses and encourages the expression of all that is natural to adolescent development—rebellion, defiance, and specialness—yet it lacks a positive, rational framework and totally disregards relational, social, and religious boundaries and values.

Why do young people get involved? For some it's simply a way to become visible, to get attention. Others see dabbling in the occult as a way to express themselves or assert independence. But to many teachers, pastors, law-enforcement people, parents, and even mental-health professionals, those who practice Satanism are a frightening mystery—and that fear gives adolescents the power they lust after. When a neighborhood, city, or individuals gets up in arms at the sight of satanic symbols, these adults play right into the young people's hands. It then becomes easier and easier for the teens to gain control over family, peers, school environment, or even community, through intimidation. (For ways to understand and to reach out to Satanists, *see* chapters 8 and 9.)

As they create their own world so also adolescents use their own imaginations and make up their own rules for the practice of Satanism. Self-styled Satanism is a "homemade" organization that differs from school to school and community to community, although most youth have read *The Satanic Bible*. They usually become involved in drug, alcohol, and sexual abuse. Rituals may include homosexuality, promiscuous heterosexuality, alcohol and drug abuse, killing and mutilating animals, and as mentioned earlier, murder.

These Satanists are frequently teenagers who read books, watch movies, or listen to records; they see sex, violence, drug use, and Satanism as marketable commodities. Often they attempt to imitate a favorite writer, actor, or rock band and create their own version of Satanism. How-to books like LaVey's *The Satanic Bible* are available in bookstores. Heavy-metal music and videos with satanic themes are very influential. So are the readily available hallucinogens, which distort the distinction between the ego and one's fantasy personality.

As a result, when some young people begin to put together their own black mass, they quickly exceed the boundaries. On the pretext of "come to a party," they may lure younger children to a ritual.

The older children quickly begin to abuse the younger ones. Fear and blood are key ingredients. Satanism sees blood as the life force, so self-styled practitioners begin to sacrifice birds and small animals. Drinking a mixture of blood and urine supposedly empowers them to endure the pain of receiving the identifying tattoo and to commit an illegal act—which must have witnesses, in order to cement the bond of silence. Taken to the extreme, death—that of a victim or oneself—becomes the perfect and ultimate sacrifice to Satan.

For the most part, self-styled Satanists are white, middle-class males. They tend to be intelligent and curious but are often underachievers; they tend to be loners; and they usually have difficulty with normal peer relationships. Minority adolescents, incidentally, learn early on that there is no free lunch. Because of a generally lower socioeconomic status, they use gangs to meet the same needs.

Religious Satanism

Anton LaVey's *The Satanic Bible*, published in 1969 and dedicated to such diverse people as P. T. Barnum, Mark Twain, Nietzsche, Howard Hughes, Marilyn Monroe, and Jayne Mansfield, contains the philosophy of the Church of Satan and describes satanic rituals, invocations, and prayers.

The Church of Satan does not seek members and "carefully screens" those who desire to join. LaVey says he wants only "the elite" in his church. Lifetime memberships in the church cost $100. LaVey's newsletter, *The Cloven Hoof*, is mailed to 2,000 people.

Sociologists who have studied LaVey's church say many of its members had serious childhood problems such as alcoholic parents, broken homes, or guilt-ridden fundamentalist upbringings. Most of them are very strongly egotistic persons, who believe that, except for themselves, the world is full of idiots and fools.

The central rite of *religious Satanism* is the black mass. The altar is a naked female, preferably a virgin, and the younger the better: an unbaptized child is perfect. Black candles are used, and the leaders—a former priest or minister, if possible, with a prostitute as his assistant—are both robed in black. A crucifix is held upside down, the Lord's Prayer is recited backwards, blood replaces wine in the chalice, and flesh is substituted for the bread. The host is consecrated in Satan's name.

In many such groups, the rituals are held under the influence of drugs: scopolamine, belladonna, curare, phenobarbital, and sodium Amytal to induce a trance. Then follow the acts of initiation and worship: pain as an offering, sex acts to bond, the secrecy oath unto death, and a criminal act—drug running, theft, or vandalism—to "prove oneself." The participant may lie inside a casket with a decomposed body in order to become comfortable with death; learn that goats' heads and other animal parts, especially hearts, and human blood and urine and feces have power; and practice hexes and curses and then cremate everything left over, so no trace of the ritual remains.

Why do people engage in such rituals? Evil and innocent suffering are facts in this world, and since people appear unable to do much about them, religious Satanism offers a way, if not to control, then at least to be in league with evil. Participation in deviant occultism becomes a path for dealing with life's problems and expressing one's identity. When a person looks for a higher power, it can be found in a good God or an evil spirit: Take your choice.

Religious Satanists share a number of characteristics with self-styled Satanists.

1. The groups tend to be male dominated. Satanists generally scorn women and use them as sex objects.
2. They prefer to emphasize the negative side of philosophical dualism, what normative religion calls bad is actually good—and vice versa.
3. They are secretive. Everything is done in darkness. Since Satanists have a fear of prosecution, no one knows how many groups there are.
4. Substance abuse—particularly of mind-altering drugs, which increase a sense of grandiosity and reduce inhibitions—has become a universal feature of satanic practice. It has been estimated that 98 percent of the rituals are performed while under the influence of a substance.
5. The initiation ceremony, a common feature of rituals, includes some sort of assault against innocence and features acts that dehumanize and profane.
6. Both groups use deliberate programming. It incorpo-

rates the use of threats (from, "We'll tell the cops," to, "Satan will get you!"); fear (assurances of the death of the person or others); and the implantation of trigger mechanisms (words, sounds, smells, and even thoughts).

7. Trigger mechanisms include signs and symbols. When Satanists see the "sign of the Beast" (*666*), the cross of confusion, the rose croix, and the eye in triangle (a symbol of secrecy), they are conditioned to affirm the triumph of matter over spirit, just as Christians are conditioned to affirm the triumph of spirit over matter, good over evil, when they see the cross of Jesus. Satanists have deliberately reversed the original intent of Christian symbols—which they see as signs of bondage—to make them affirmations of the freedom that only death can make final. Thus the cross, which for Christians stands for salvation and goodness, is inverted by Satanists to signify earthiness and evil.

Membership in such groups is voluntary, elitist, and exclusive, and provides a sense of belonging different from what the religious Satanists experienced elsewhere in society. One scientist who has examined the groups from within observed that most members had a common characteristic: a behavioral trait that placed them outside the social norm. For these people, the satanic rituals served to build ego and lessen anxiety and guilt. So we must not, I think, write this off as "crazy religious stuff": It must be taken seriously, especially since, while the simple practice of their religion is legal, many of the acts are not.

Multigenerational Satanism

The third type, according to some investigations, is *multigenerational Satanism*, the most difficult to discuss because the groups are unconnected, and because the practices are so bizarre that they strain credibility.

There are reports of family groups in which a two-year-old is starved for days, brought into a black mass—presided over by a male relative—and in a span of three hours, endures emotional trauma, sexual abuse, mutilation of beloved pet animals, the sight of other children being abused, and threats to his or her life.

Such people have come to believe that good is bad and bad is good, that the initiate robed in white is in need of purification, and those in black are the favored ones. Their value system has been so undermined that their sense of self is completely altered.

Men in these groups view women totally as producers of children. At a propitious astrological moment, the act of impregnation by the high priest can only take place on the altar, after the female has been purified by days or weeks of fasting, hours of repeated flushing of every body cavity, and the *pain*staking (literally) enactment of proper ritual.

These groups, it is charged, will deliberately fatten a female, toward the end of her second trimester, in order to mask the pregnancy; they hide her from view as the due date approaches and induce the birth; they will sacrifice the days-old child as the most innocent and perfect gift to Satan, then cremate all that remains of a human being whose arrival was never recorded and who, so far as the rest of society will ever know, never existed.

While I have received numerous phone calls from

women who claim to have been used as "breeders" in such satanic groups, I have not found any evidence to support their claims. Many of the reports surface when women claiming such terrible abuse go into psychological counseling. I keep an open mind on the subject, but so far I am skeptical about these claims.

Why would anyone stay in such a group? Part of the answer is that it is their religion. They believe that their god has power over life and that by participating in the rituals they can also participate in the power. Part of the answer, too, lies in the dehumanizing conditioning or programming to which the group subjects initiates from the beginning—often from a preconscious age. The conditioning takes many forms:

Social: They are severely restricted in relationships beyond the family.

Spiritual: They believe, *Satan owns you, body and soul*.

Physical: When a mother has died, the group initiates the prepubescent daughter to take her place.

Psychic: When a member is intensely attuned, he or she believes, *They will hear me everywhere*. (This is similar to fears induced in members of destructive cults like the Family of Love.)

Sexual: As in the case in which a razor blade attached to an electric drill was inserted into the vagina of the girl on the altar, and she was told that sex with anyone outside the family would pull the trigger.

Religious: Lent and Good Friday are high holy times for Satanists, who may cut and maim one another to defile the image of Jesus, who was recognized, after the resurrection, by the scars in his hands and side.

A third reason people stay in these groups is the confusion of identity that arises from the enforced dual socialization. Simultaneously they exist in the normative world and in the deviant world. What they do in church on Sunday, in the basement or the barn on Wednesday, and in school five days a week are all part of a single experience. As a result they disassociate, split, or pop out of body from time to time. Some therapists at Rush-Presbyterian Hospital, Chicago, have reported that 90 percent of their multiple personality disorder patients have multigenerational Satanism in their pasts. Frankly, I doubt the facticity of most of these supposed MPD cases. Most seem based on the book *Michelle Remembers*, a volume that offers no existential proof of its assertions.[1] Beyond the MPD characterization, however, no profile of these people is available.

Cultic Satanism

Cultic Satanism generally involves adults, or adults who also involve youth and children, who perform underground satanic rituals of a predatory nature. It often involves homosexual activity, child sex, and heterosexual promiscuity; alcohol and drug abuse; the sacrifice and mutilation of animals and, on several occasions, murder.

These Satanists are involved in criminal activities such as drug trafficking, kidnapping, pornography, and human ritual murders. In July, 1984, the *New York Times* reported on one of these Satanic cults, the Knights of the Black Circle. The group, consisting of twenty teenage members, held meetings on Long Island, sacrificed animals, and used hallucinogenic drugs such as angel dust. During one of their four-hour rituals, a seventeen-year-old was tortured and killed. Later, one of the two jailed suspects hanged himself. The article reported the police were investigating the influence of so-called heavy-metal rock music on the members of this group.

Chapter 1 discussed these criminally oriented cults, along with the murderous activity of some self-styled or teenage Satanists. Under the influence of drug abuse and the sense of alienation from family, school, church, and community that grow like flowers of evil in many small towns and suburban areas of North America, dabblers can quickly grow into cults.

Satanism, whether individually practiced or group oriented, is an example of alienation, a symbol of rejection of things as they are perceived to be in late twentieth-century America. The countercultural revolution of the 1960s and 1970s heavily influenced both teenage Satanists and satanic cults. With it has come massive sociological changes that have contributed enormously to the kinds of things therapists are now seeing. Besides a crisis of confidence in government and authority, brought on by Watergate and the war in Vietnam, we have seen:

> An unprecedented increase in the availability, use, and abuse of illicit and psychoactive drugs.
>
> Breakdown of traditional family values and structures, replaced by multiple families, unsupervised children, and absence of parental authority.
>
> An upheaval in sexual mores, with confusion over sexual role models and identity.
>
> Shifts in educational patterns along with teachers' loss of authority and the ability to discipline.

Extreme emphasis on narcissism and self-aggrandizement: "If it feels good, do it"; "Look out for Number 1"; and encouragement of immediate gratification.

Promotion of violence, availability of weapons, films, catalogs, and "winning through intimidation" in popular psychology.

Heavy-metal music, breaking taboos of sound, sight, and lyrics, from Ozzy Osbourne, KISS, and Motley Crue, to teens making the "sign of the horns" at a Slayer concert.

As Anton LaVey observes, Satan became a symbol challenging the established order, with its traditional value system. The attacks on patriarchy, the position of the male, the father, made by extreme feminism also called into question the traditional family structure and the symbol of God as Father.

Caribbean and African Cults

For over two hundred years the United States has been influenced by religious and magical ideas from Africa, the Caribbean, and Asia. The practice of slavery brought West African practices to the Deep South and to the Caribbean islands. Many Latin American ideas and practices came into the United States from Mexico. Participation in Asian trade and wars made Oriental religions prominent in America after World War II.

The Yoruba tribal religion is the common background of Santeria, Macumba, Candomblé, Lucumi, Santuario, and Palo Mayombe. This influence has multiplied in the United States since the Mariel boat lifts of 1980.

All African-background groups have a common element in ritual sacrifices, called "matanza." Blood offerings are the most important feature for all these groups. Animals sacrificed mainly include chickens, goats, and turtles.

In addition to religious, cultic, and self-styled Satanism, various forms of occult practice appear across the United States, Canada, and Mexico, as well as in Cuba, the Caribbean islands, and Latin America.[2] These groups include:

1. *Voodoo* (or properly *voodun*) has an Ibo tribe (Nigerian) background, overlaid with older French Roman Catholicism, in Haiti. The zombie cult and sophisticated drug and herb use mark this group. It is found in Miami, New York City, and elsewhere in the United States.

2. *Santeria* ("the Saints") comes from the Yoruba tribe (southwest Nigerian), mingled with the practices of old Spanish Roman Catholicism, in Cuba. In the United States there are about 80,000 Santeria followers in southern Florida, as well as others in Boston, New York, Philadelphia, Chicago, Detroit, San Francisco, Los Angeles, New Orleans, and elsewhere.

3. *Hoodoo* is United States southern black folk magic, involving the "root doctor" or "conjure man." It is witchcraft, and its background is English, not African.

4. *Brujeria* is the sorcery cult of northern Mexico and the American Southwest. It mixes Santeria-like elements with old European magic and the sorcery or witch cults of native American (Indian) tribes. It has some similarities to the black witch cults of the Pueblo and Navaho Indian tribes. The Navahos, for example, had and have a great fear of these witch cults. Indeed, the large Indian reservations of the Southwest are now disturbed by satanic activ-

ity and have recently held seminars to try to combat it.

5. *Macumba* is a Brazilian movement in which African tribal religion and the old Portuguese Roman Catholicism fused. In it, the African elements are purer and more dominant than in Santeria. *Macumba* means "to sacrifice to the gods."

6. *Quimbanda* is Brazilian black magic, the sorcery cult of Macumba.

7. *Pajelanca* is an Afro-Brazilian cult of the Amazon religion.

8. *Palo Mayombe* is a purer African sorcery cult, probably the same as Pajelanca. It is, perhaps, a loose term applicable to the Matamoros group, although that group seems almost pure West African.

9. *Candomblé* is an Afro-Brazilian cult, found in Bahía state.

10. *Lucumi* is a variant of Macumba.

11. *Umbanda* is the same as Macumba. It is found in Rio de Janeiro.

12. *The Brownsville, Texas–Matamoros, Mexico, drug cult* is *not* Voodoo, *not* Santeria, *not* Hoodoo; nor is it Yoruba religion. It is most closely related to a sorcery cult, that is, to African black magic. It shares some similarities with Santeria (from Cuba) and to Brujeria (from Mexico). In that Brujeria is a black-magic cult, the drug cult is closest to this New World "left-hand path." Since it is a malevolent cult that appeals to evil spirits, not to God or the saints, for protection, it is perfectly proper to refer to it as satanic. A classic example of such a cult existed among black rebel soldiers in the Congo rebellion of the 1960s. The magic then was designed to protect the rebels against bullets and make them "invisible" to their enemies.

The Brownsville–Matamoros cult is a New World variant of a West African sorcery cult. Sorcerers gain power over spirits by elaborate rituals and sacrifices; witches come by their supposed powers naturally. Therefore the cult leader (or "patron" or "father") is a sorcerer, not a witch. It remains to be seen if the woman involved functions as a witch or a sorcerer.

How did this strongly African cult get here? Undoubtedly through the influence of Cuban involvement in Angola and in other parts of Africa. Over 30,000 Cuban soldiers a year served in Africa for over a decade—perhaps for twenty years.

Major points of agreement exist between the Matamoros cult evidence and West African sorcery (as well as in the general worldview of Yoruba religion, which forms the background of Santeria):

1. Belief in sorcerers and witches is universal in West Africa. These individuals are always malevolent and evil, playing the same role as Satanists in a Judeo-Christian context; that is, they are destructive and stand for the breakdown of the community.
2. Every occupation has its special kind of ceremonies and sacrifices: Farmers owe certain sacrifices; those who want to win love, another kind. But what sacrifice is appropriate to drug smugglers, involved in an illegal profession?
3. Anyone requesting the help of a spirit must do so in terms of an equitable contract; for example, a chicken is given for a safe journey, but a larger sacrifice is required for the death of an enemy.
4. The sorcerer is a *babalawos*, in Yoruba, meaning "fa-

ther of secrets." This is similar to *padrone*, "godfa-
ther" or "boss," in Mexican speech.

5. Rather than having a single evil person, West African
   thought sees each sorcerer or witch as the fundamen-
   tal source of evil. Therefore, the cult leaders *are* the
   devil. Sorcerers are generally men, and witches are
   generally women. Both are always malicious. Those
   taken in by sorcerers are said to crave human flesh.
6. Sorcerers commonly make sacrifices for protection
   against physical as well as spiritual powers.
7. Divination, or forecasting the future, is done by
   rituals—the evidence of these divinations seems to be
   present at the Matamoros site.
8. The ritual items found at the Matamoros site confirm
   an evaluation of the proceedings there as derived
   from a West African sorcery cult:

   Chicken parts: Yes or no answers are gotten by cutting off a chicken's head and letting the body flop
   around. If it ends up on its back, the answer is yes; if
   it ends up on its stomach, the answer is no.

   A pottery bowl full of cheap gold beads: These objects
   are picked up randomly in the left hand. Even numbers yield one line; odd numbers yield two lines. This
   yields 256 patterns, like the 64 hexagrams of the ancient Chinese I Ching, which unfolds its patterns or
   hexagrams when one casts yarrow sticks or thin stalks
   or three coins. This is definitely a West African form
   of divination. The pennies found in the bowl with
   human and animal parts and sticks probably were
   used in a form of divination like this as well.

   A caldron: Generally, this is where the *palero* stores
   "secrets." It might contain "sacred" dirt, coins,

blood, and human bones. At Matamoros, coins, human bones, a horseshoe, chicken parts, and a turtle shell, plus other things, were found. The caldron, called a *nganga* or *prenda*, is *the* source of power in rituals.

Cigars: These, found at Matamoros, are used to attract the "deity" in all such sorcery groups.

Copper: This symbolizes Oshunm, an orisha (or deity) from Africa. Copper pennies were found in the caldron at Matamoros.

Fire: Chango, the chief Yoruba deity, is invoked in sorcery. This deity is associated with thunder, fire, and cigars.

Horseshoes: These symbolize the warrior god, Ogyum. A horseshoe was found at the Matamoros site.

Pennies: Often seven pennies are used to symbolize the seven African power deities.

Sanctuary: The shed at Matamoros was a sanctuary or *Idbodu.*

Brains: The brains found in the caldron probably show that a skull was put into the mixture, as brains are generally left in the skull so it can "think."

Sticks: In general, sticks are stuck into the ground around or in any sacrifice. Sticking a twig in the caldron may be an actual or symbolic rite of eating (partaking of or "communioning" with) the power believed to be in the caldron.

A sword or machete: Black magic or Palo Mayombe especially uses these. A machete is a common item in Mexico, but clearly one killed Mark Kilroy.

It should not be overlooked that the Matamoros cult member who confessed spoke of sacrificing to "the devil." Nor should the goat's head (associated with the devil) or the inverted crosses tattooed on at least one cult member be forgotten. This hybrid cult was fundamentally designed to be satanic, that is, evil.

In the United States, in addition to various forms of Satanism, a number of black occultic groups of European background exist, although they often form a syncretistic (and illogical) mix, combining with elements from Asia, Africa, the Middle East, Ancient Egypt, pagan Scandinavia, and native American cultures. These include:

1. *Witchcraft of many varieties.* Generally this worships or reverences nature as the Great Mother and mystery. There are many feminist witches, but witchcraft also includes covens that attempt to preserve Celtic traditions (Druids) or other systems from the past. Most witchcraft is said to be "white" or nonhostile. There are "black," or hostile, evil witches, too.
2. *Neopagans.* These often overlap with witches but seem more inclined to try to recreate an ancient religion, such as the Druids (Celts), Norse, Welsh, or ancient Egyptian practices. This is a small group, perhaps 40,000 people at most.
3. *Ceremonial and/or sex-magic cults.* The OTO and other groups that stem from Aleister Crowley primarily make up this form. Crowley attempted to create a psychologized, bisexually based system of elaborate rituals called "Thelemic magic."

All the various cults of Latin American and African background developed out of indigenous attempts to combine pagan religions and superstitions of African and native American origins, and in some cases, with Christianity. The destructive occultic groups, such as Crowley's OTO and LaVey's Satanism, developed out of Western and Middle Eastern backgrounds, in direct opposition to Christianity. Neopaganism and some forms of witchcraft today claim to grow out of recovered pre-Christian roots. In general, we can say that all are pagan or heretical movements and some (such as Palo Mayombe and some forms of Satanism) include violently destructive and criminal behavior.

As to whether any groups not calling themselves satanic should be equated with Satanism, I think this is a matter of semantics. Clearly, Palo Mayombe and Crowley's practices are satanic in any Christian use of the word. In point of social scientific fact, only those groups calling themselves satanic can be grouped together as Satanism. I prefer to use the term *destructive occultism* to cover all cases of groups that seek to work evil or perform sacrifices of living creatures.

5
A Devilish Attraction

Over the past two decades, social commentators, law-enforcement personnel, mental-health professionals, and some conservative clergy have noticed an upsurge of occult and pagan groups. These include covens of witches, religious assemblies confessing pagan beliefs, and satanic cults.

In interviews, participants in pagan and witchcraft circles explain these developments in terms of dissatisfaction with the Christian churches and Christian moral teachings. This may well be true of some extreme feminists and of those drawn to pagan rituals based on nature, but it emphatically is not the reason why some persons choose Satanism. People attracted to the dark lord of evil tend to have problems relating to others and to the "real" world of social obligations. Such people choose Satanism as an arena in which to act out their personal fantasies in unbridled hedonism, utter materialism ("going for the gold"), and in rituals and behaviors that inflate their very damaged egos. Becoming Satanists leads many of these inadequate or antisocial personalities into self-abuse (slashing their arms as sacrifices to Satan) and to suicidal behavior. Other, perhaps more damaged personalities, act out their hostilities and gain a sense of superiority by harming others.

The church may, indeed, have failed many people today and in the past, but a sense of dissatisfaction with Christianity alone does not lead one into Satanism. Insecure personalities, weak egos, and indulgent selfishness are more likely the reasons a small minority worships the Beast. Satanism is the practice of selfishness, of self-indulgence, of life only in and for the present moment. It encourages no sense of responsibility for others or for the community or for the future. The triumph of the sick will make Satanism attractive because it promises that the strong will exert total control over the weak. In the ultimate, philosophical sense, then Satanism is the opposite of the teachings of orthodox Christian churches.

Going From Bad to Worse to Hell

According to data released by the federal government in its contemporary campaign or "war" on drugs, some 42 million Americans have at least tried illegal drugs. Since the population of the United States is about 260 million, this means over one-sixth of the American people have used, if only experimentally, marijuana, cocaine, heroin, hashish, opium, "crack," "crank," "speed," "meth," "acid," peyote, and other mind-altering drugs. Most of these experimenters have, presumably, only tried marijuana, but a significant number have indulged in the death-threatening hard drugs, despite warnings and the threat of legal prosecution.

These literally staggering statistics clearly point up the nature of contemporary North American society: one of utter self-indulgence in which selfish people will brook no limits on their personal pleasure. Perhaps we should display this drug-abuse statistic next to divorce statistics. That figure would say something, too, about shallow characters who cannot keep their vows, who will not endure any discomfort in order to hold a marriage, a family, together. Combined, these sets of statistics would provide a formula that explains "the me generation" and go far toward explicating the current cultural moral morass that is the background and precondition for the rise of Satanism.

We live in an occult-saturated society. The pounding beat of heavy-metal music, which often gives homage to the devil in its lyrics, is heard all over the continent. Films, in public movie houses and in VCRs in millions of homes, spread occult interests and themes. Fantasy games and fantasy literature invite the susceptible young into a world of magic, curses, and demons. Illegal drugs, seemingly available everywhere to people of all ages, combine with heavy alcohol consumption to produce millions of people in a semipermanent state of altered consciousness. For hundreds of thousands, the doors of perception are broken down, and thousands pour through those doors, emotionally going from bad to worse—and for some, all the way to hell. The New Age is merely a misnomer for a social climate that promotes being out of touch with reality as the only way to live. Numbed by the experience of seeking every pleasure, tricked by perverse thinking that names every vice a virtue, people suffering from this cultural brainwashing and from the results of their own wrong conduct cannot understand what is happening to them. If Satan is the father of lies, the deceiver of the human race, as traditional theology declares him to be (and as I believe him to be), then it is no exaggeration to suggest that the one Jesus called the prince of this world is indeed the ruler of this place, this time. Can we wonder, then, that some among us would move from "sympathy for the devil" to expectant reverence of his dark majesty? As some thrash-metal rock groups have it, echoing the secret satanic rites enacted by a tiny minority, "Satan rules! Satan lives! NATAS NEMA."

Media of the Devil?

Too much ink has been used to heavily denounce heavy-metal rock music and fantasy games like Dungeons & Dragons for it to be necessary to do much more than point out the basically faddish and escapist nature of both youth-directed activities. In the cycle of ever-changing fads of "who's in" and "who's out," many young people listen to heavy-metal music and play an occasional game of Dungeons & Dragons without any specific ill effects. The greatest damage done to this majority of youth is the physical injury done to their eardrums by loud music and the terrific drain on their parents' pocketbooks for the awfully expensive concert tickets, tapes and CDs, and various fantasy-game components such youths continually want to buy. But some American youth can become psychologically addicted to the more gross thrash-metal bands and/or to the continuous flight into guided fantasy of Dungeons & Dragons and related games. All of us are immersed in a sea of cultural occultism; youth and others who succumb to heavy metal, horror films, and fantasy games drown intellectually in the perversity of the New Age.

Occult Filmmaking. The films that glorify Satan have been coming out for a long time. *Rosemary's Baby* is two decades old. *The Omen, Omen II,* and sequels have been around for years. *Salem's Lot* and numerous other movies about witches, Satanists, vampires, and assorted monsters are staples of the VCR-using public. Perhaps the latest occult film of any degree of power is *The Believers.* Constanzo, the black sorcerer who led the Matamoros cult in ritual human sacrifices, declared that he patterned his group on this movie.

Dozens of mostly "B" movies have occult themes: *Baron Blood, Blacula, Countess Dracula, Daughters of Satan, Vampire Circus, The Possession of Joel Delaney, An American Werewolf in London, Teen Wolf, The Serpent and the Rainbow,* and, of course, the numerous *Friday the 13th* films and the *Nightmare on Elm Street* series. Even very young children routinely rent horror and occult films. The video store and VCR provide all the conditioning into occultism the most devout Satanist could wish.

Does Satan Have All the Good Music?

The flashing of the "horns" (first and fourth fingers upright, with the second and third fingers folded over the palm) at rock concerts, the emphasis on black garments and chains, and lyrics encouraging the recognition of Satan all contribute to the conditioning of already alienated young people into antisocial acts. Whether or not certain rock stars are actual Satanists is immaterial, because many rock singers hold Satan and the utter inversion of traditional values up as the way youth should go in their lives. Whether or not they do it purely to garner popularity by pandering to the feeling of hostility in teenagers makes no difference. The destructive effect is the same as if such singers were dedicated "evangelists" of the antichrist.

A 1989 murder-suicide demonstrates the terrible consequences of occult conditioning through music, books, and drugs:

> David Olive and Phillip Gomiser, Jr., inseparable friends, fans of heavy metal music and problems to their parents, at 15 were tired of life.
>
> So they picked a quiet spot in the woods, gouged their epitaphs on homemade styrofoam tombstones and played a Led Zeppelin tape in a boom box while one shot the other, then shot himself. Their decomposed bodies were found Wednesday night, eight days after Olive's mother reported him missing to police, west of Lantana.
>
> The deaths of Olive and Gomiser have left their families shaken and wondering what drove the boys to shut them out, then kill themselves.
>
> "He was so distant, and he just kept getting farther and farther away," Elaine Olive said Thursday, recalling the last few months of her son's life. "In the last couple of weeks you couldn't get more than a grunt out of him."
>
> Their tombstones bore the inscription "R.I.P.," along with their initials and symbols that Palm Beach County sheriff's spokesman Bob Ferrell said may have been Satanic. "One of the boys had a lot of pentagrams and that type of drawings in his house."

> Elaine Olive said her son had given no indication
> that he was involved in satanism. She said she also
> would not allow him to listen to heavy metal music in
> her house.
>
> Said Phillip Gomiser, Sr.: "I could talk to him, but
> I think his friends had more influence with him than
> I did. . . . He got into some trouble a while ago and I
> took all of his heavy metal music tapes away."[1]

The use of drugs by so many stars in the popular music world is an equally unquestioned bad influence on youth—and on the public in general. Rock music invariably seems to go along with some sort of drug abuse among its practitioners. The potent combination of drug abuse and hostile, antiestablishment, satanic themes and art (on record covers) is overwhelming in its impact on the more disturbed among contemporary youth. Satanism, from the dabbling stage to the criminal stage, is always linked with substance abuse. The fact that the Matamoros cult was formed to smuggle marijuana into the United States does not lack meaning. Drug misuse destroys the moral character of the abuser. Satanism represents the antimorality of those in whom the socially conditioned conscience has never developed or has been extinguished.

A Visit to a Coven

The drug-intoxicated hedonistic quest for more and more sensual thrills is well illustrated by the following account of a visit to a party put on by black occultists. I owe this opportunity to the good offices of a professor at a large state university. Some of the participants were students in his department.

Imagine yourself walking down a major street of a medium-sized city with fewer than 100,000 residents. A small, very well-known liberal-arts college lies on your left; to the right opens a sedate residential street. You turn right and walk under the graceful old trees that line the sidewalk. On the right is a brick bungalow, the home of a nationally known psychiatrist. Just down the way, the chairman of a department of a major university makes his home. Hardly the place to go witch hunting? Hardly, and yet across the street, one house down, is the location of a coven. Five people—three men and two women—and all of them witches.

We cross the street and climb the stairs of an old mansion that has an air of tiredness. It is not a run-down building. The house is painted and swept, but it has lost its glory. Now it is divided into apartments, two up and two down. We go upstairs and knock at a door. It opens at our rap, of its own weight. The door is not locked, nor has it a lock at all. The rooms of the coven stand open to the world.

What rooms these are! There are five, all differently decorated. In the room we enter, dolls, painted and distorted and torn, hang everywhere. A crushed skull stands on a shelf. A coffee table supports a birdcage in the middle of the room. Inside the cage is a painted doll, rather than a bird. From time to time someone takes a sword and torments the doll, all the while calling it "Cosmic Charlie."

One corner contains a fireplace. A gas log is burning there. Several other persons are seated in front of this fire, "grooving" or "flashing" on the flickering gas light. The people in this room are almost completely "stoned," intoxicated on drugs.

Someone greets us and hands us the skull. This is a grotesque item, old, brown, with the jaw missing and with a crushed-in line running from the right eye to the top of the skull. The boy who has given us the skull tells us that it is the remains of a murder victim, dug up in an adjoining city by black cultic friends who sent it on to them as a present. We are offered a marijuana cigarette, decline it, and wander into another room. Walking through the crowd of guests in the dim light, we are struck by the wild expressions on the faces of some of the people present. A tall, beautiful, black-haired girl sways back and forth as if hypnotized. Incidentally, some of the guests are rather distantly "tripped out" on LSD.

The next room is brightly painted and at first reminds us of a little girl's room. There is one significant difference—all the furniture in this room has been very carefully bolted to the ceiling. Brightly glowing colors cover the table, four chairs, dishes, silverware, glasses, and flowers that hang suspended from the ceiling. This witty, amusingly decorated room lightens our outlook, and some of the sense of evil that we felt in the other room falls away from us.

With the next room some of that foreboding returns, because of its color as well as on account of the direction in which it drives our thoughts. It is a small room, painted completely black, a deep, ebony, shining black, from floor to ceiling. There is only one object in the room, a brass bed; all of it is painted black, too, except for the large rails at the head and foot, which glow richly in the light falling from the next room. There are no lights and no other objects in the "bedroom."

We walk back toward the front room and become aware of exotic music coming from a record player hidden somewhere in a dark corner. A few of the people in the larger room are moving back and forth to the music, dancing to the weird sounds. From their behavior, we would judge that at least some of these people are homosexuals.

The people at this party mentioned their connection with other black occult groups in neighboring cities. The cult members seemed to share the following characteristics: All of them were young, under thirty for the most part, with high school and some college education; almost all were out of college or high school and working at white collar jobs; all seemed to be single, but many were living together, often with several men and women sharing the same apartment. The use of wine, beer, marijuana, and drugs, including psychedelics, seemed universal among them. While totally alienated from their society, they seemed apolitical. All had turned in upon themselves, fascinated by their internal contradictions, living by a sensationalist hedonism. For them, evil was more fun than good, and they derived great pleasure from shocking and frightening the more passive types of "cool" students who lived in other apartments in their area. One such very upset student who visited the coven said he believed they would like to make a human sacrifice, just to see what that trip would be like.

The Lure of Pleasure:
Sex, Drugs, and Rock 'n' Roll

Paul Banner, senior criminology instructor at the South Carolina Justice Academy, labels one motivation for involvement in Satanism "physical/mental." Someone else said, "It's fun," and of course, it may seem like fun, at first, for antisocial youth. The promise of sex, drugs, alcohol, and the feelings of superiority over persons frightened by occultic behavior may make Satanism very attractive to alienated young people. This "fun" element may explain why so many youth who end up in destructive occultism have a deep background in fantasy games like Dungeons & Dragons. What starts out as a lark becomes an alternative reality in which such young people work out their sense of hostility and alienation from family and community. In a few, the distinction between fantasy and reality becomes completely blurred.

The lure of drugs is probably the most potent recruiting tool Satanism has today. Experimenting, adventurous, and alienated young people do "try" drugs of every description, from alcohol to pot to the most dangerous street chemicals. The pleasures of the flesh represent the real values of many such youths' parents. They have grown up watching their parents drink alcohol at every opportunity, use tranquilizers, and in some cases, smoke marijuana or use cocaine. Such youngsters think older people are being hypocritical when they urge youth to "just say no," and they are not wrong in their assessment. Those parents may have been taught different values as children, although they do not live by them, but the youngsters may have had no such values conditioning. For them, the pleasure principle is the only standard of morality they know.

The three basic motivations for involvement in Satanism include:

Social/political motivations. A form of the black mass performed as early as the fourteenth century was primarily a burlesque or parody of the Christian rite; it was attended by "the mass," by common people such as the serfs. Its purpose was twofold.

1. It was a way to let off steam by ridiculing the religion of the landowners and priests who controlled them.
2. It was an appeal to "another god." Satan was often referred to as the "god of the serfs" and the "god of liberty."

The Inquisition's attempt to weed out "heretics" was as much an attempt to prevent revolution as it was to promote theological purity. Satanism, for some people, represents a way to show opposition to the "establishment."

Physical/mental motivations. As stated before, the lure of pleasure draws many young people.

Carl Raschke says "the satanic mindset is not 'religion' in the regular sense of the word, but a mystification of the most corrupt secular passions and values."[2] Anton LaVey, author of *The Satanic Bible*, in his public pronouncements about Satanism, merely presented an artificial religious handle for good old-fashioned lust and libertinism.

The general practice of Satanism provides three areas of attraction:

1. Gratification of the flesh
2. Gratification of the ego
3. Power

Spiritual motivations. Some feel that Satanism is a viable way of getting supernatural help because:

1. They are too distant from the "good God" to have any hope of reaching him.

2. The "good God" and his virtues, such as beauty, joy, and so on, are essentially impractical.
3. It seems easier to catch the notice of an evil god than a good one.

It is fanatical to believe that every youth who plays fantasy games or enjoys heavy-metal rock music is into occultism, but young people found engaged in destructive occultism usually are hyperinvolved in thrash metal, like Ozzy Osborne, Slayer, Venom, and Poison. The lyrics, dress, symbols, and life-styles of these heavy-metal singers and performers make Satanism attractive to many young people, from a very early age. Join the sadistic lyrics and blatantly perverse sexuality of these rock bands to the intoxication of alcohol, pot or hard drugs, and you have very heavy conditioning that might well tip a teenager into antisocial behavior. Satanism and drugs always go together.

Toward the Year A.D. 2000

Why are people attracted to Satanism today? Because all the old standards of conduct and beliefs about God and his relation to the world have been displaced or destroyed in millions of people. The news of the death of God is at the same time the announcement of the birth of Satan. Erosion of the older traditional beliefs has gone on for over one hundred years in America and for much longer in Western Europe. The extinguishment of conscience is not of recent vintage. For over fifty years the pleasure principle has been urged as a desirable substitute for one's duty. Long ago the quest for self-knowledge and self-fulfillment became more important than the quest for God and to do his will, even among the most committed church members.

Yet there is more to Satanism's attraction today. Two opposite but equal motivations become obvious upon even superficial observation. The first, the promise of fun, is fleshly, seemingly positive and promising. The second is spiritual, negative, a rumor of endings; it is the fear induced by a culturewide attraction for apocalypticism in eschatology. Twentieth-century people seek hidden "signs of the times" for the soon-approaching end of history.

The Christian sectarian end-of-the-age syndrome is often met with in discussions with those caught up in the occult. As we draw nearer the year A.D. 2000, we may confidently expect even more such activity in North America. We have already seen it in end-of-the-age fundamentalists (*Satan Is Alive and Well on Planet Earth*, by Hal Lindsey,[3] is a clear example of this outlook) and the cultic occultists.

Millennial superstition and apocalyptic thoughts haunt Anglo-American society. Over the centuries, no other segment of civilization has spawned so many end-of-the-age movements as Britain, the United States, and the British Commonwealth. The underground current of an imagined, feared, or welcomed end to things as they are runs deep in the English-speaking mind. From the time of the Diggers, Levelers, and Fifth Monarchy Men of Oliver Cromwell's Protestant sectarian army, to the Darbyites and their dispensationalism, to the announcement of the end of history and the second coming by the Millerites and the several branches of Adventists in America, the millennial idea runs clear and bright. In the twentieth century, too, the idea that the second coming is upon us formed parts of the revivals that crisscrossed the country, as well as of the crusades, radio, and later television broadcasts of Billy Graham, Oral Roberts, and their imitators. It is not surprising, then, that the one "religious" element we can discern in much Satanism today is this millennial, end-of-the-age motif.

Charles Manson, one of the earliest destructive occultists to injure the American public, taught that "helter skelter,"[4] an Armageddon-like race war, must be fomented in America. He believed his horrible torture murders would touch off the powder keg of racial hatred and bring down contemporary society.

The first actual satanic institutional movement, "The Process Church of the Final Judgment," which influenced Manson[5] stresses the end of the world. The Process worship both God and Satan, Christ and Lucifer, hoping for the coming of a new "messiah" who will establish a millennium of love.

The Process split into two groups in 1974, one of which is even more profoundly apocalyptic. The Foundation Church of the Millennium sees the end of the world as coming around the year A.D. 2000. Believers base this prediction on biblical prophecy (in the Protestant sectarian tradition), on Nostradamus, and on psychics such as Edgar Cayce and Jean Dixon. The general idea is that mankind will destroy civilization through nuclear war. Like all millennial sects, Process believers teach that a remnant will be saved, while the majority of humanity will be destroyed and presumably damned. After the end, the believers will partake in a new beginning.

Since both groups that descend from the original Process movement worship Satan and Lucifer as well as God and Christ (they have four "gods"), the connection to Satanism is quite real, at least for some believers. Maury Terry, an investigative reporter for the Port Chester, New York, *Daily Item* and an editor of IBM Company publications, came to believe in a nationwide network of Process church members who worshiped Satan more than the other three gods of the Process pantheon. While Terry's interpretations and conclusions are controversial, his book, *The Ultimate Evil*,[6] does investigate numerous occult crimes. Terry also gives much food for thought about the occult involvement of persons like David Berkowitz (the "Son of Sam") and Charles Manson. His book contains a wealth of information on destructive occultism, including photos of ritual sites. Above all, he highlights the millennial, end-of-the-age mind-set of black occultists. Satan, however, is the new messiah in these psychotic visions, just as the movie *Rosemary's Baby* portrays a Satanic coven welcoming the satanic messiah in a parody of the Christian nativity story.

It may appear incredible that people could believe in "the second coming of Satan" and look forward with joy to the advent of an evil messiah, but some persons do. "Satan rules!" "Hail, Satan!" "The year one!" all are expressions found tattooed on people's bodies, spray painted on underpasses, and carefully painted on the walls of hidden ritual sites.

No one finds it impossible to believe that the simple faithful look with great expectation for the literal, bodily second appearing of the Lord Jesus Christ. Although many do not believe that tenet of Christianity, they respect it because the reality of its hold on human beings has been clearly demonstrated for centuries and can be seen today. Since Satanism is the inversion of Christianity, we should have no difficulty recognizing the hold this inverted belief has on the religious Satanist. There are those who look forward to a "black Christmas" as intently as any child awaits the traditional Christmas morning.

When you no longer wish to believe in God, there is no need to be alone in the universe. Belief in the pleasure principle, in sex, drugs, rock music, psychological power, and one's own superiority makes belief in the devil all too easy.

6
The Toys of the Damned: Satanic Paraphernalia and Rites

I was recently asked my advice on the request of a prisoner in a state penitentiary for the tools to perform Satanic rites. In fact, this inmate furnished a copy of a popular book that had drawings of some needed ritual objects. One was a sharp knife; another was a sword.

I asked the warden's assistant who showed me this material, "Would you want a career criminal running around inside the prison with a knife like that? Or a sword?" She smiled, and that answer may have solved the prison's problem.

Satanic paraphernalia is not just an extension of Halloween costumes and gimmicks. The tools, or better, the toys of the damned are a grim and serious business. At base, the ritual objects of Satanism reveal its origins, out of the witchcraft of the romantic reaction of the past two centuries and from the perversions of Roman Catholic liturgy by the French nobility at the time of Louis XIV. Both witchcraft and Satanism go in for secluded sites and rituals, requiring participants either to go robed in various vestments or "sky-clad" (naked), with the use of chalices, knives, wands, swords, candles (in a variety of colors), incense, fire, group concentration, and perhaps sexual activity and sacrifice.

In general, however, there is a clear line of distinction between witchcraft rituals and satanic rites, and there are ritual "objects" in Satanism that are not found among witches. Satanists prize human bones, especially skulls, and make use of body parts, corpses, live animals, and blood. The toys of the damned are grim indeed.

The items used in satanic rituals are obtained either legally or illegally. Mail-order catalogs, certain "underground" publishing houses, and occult bookstores (a long-standing element in many cities) not only provide the books that spread Satanism but also sell the tools needed in its practice. Candles, knives, chalices, swords, robes, cords, symbols—all are for sale, quite legally. There are even underground newsletters that advertise skulls and skeletons for sale, perhaps not quite so legally. Body parts, which many black occultists seem to feel are necessary in their worship, cannot be legally obtained. To obtain these skulls, fingers, and bones, Satanists rob graves and tombs. As gruesome as this sounds, grave robbing does occur; it is not just an element in a late-night horror movie. Some satanic groups have become so adept at grave robbing that they dig only near the memorial stone, at the head of the casket, and break open that end so as to remove the skull with a minimum of work. Some satanic groups earn money by doing extensive cemetery vandalism and selling the surplus "parts" to other covens by the underground grapevine. There is a real underground economy in occultism; and corpses, skulls, and other body parts are major elements in it.

The Individual Ritual Objects

The Satanic Bible describes the following objects:

1. Clothing or jewelry—This includes robes (usually black, but sometimes red or other colors) and amulets (usually with an occult or Satanic symbol on them).
2. The altar—Traditionally a nude woman is the actual altar, but she would lie on a sort of a slab of stone or metal. Almost anything could be used, but a recommended one is trapezoidal in shape, about three or four feet high and five and a half to six feet long.
3. The symbol of Baphomet, as shown here. It also goes by other names.

4. Candles—*The Satanic Bible* says to use only one white candle and the rest black. Some groups may use other colors.
5. Bell—A bell is used at the beginning and end of many

satanic rituals. It will usually have a loud, penetrating sound.

6. Chalice—A goblet, preferably silver, could be made of anything except gold.
7. Elixir—*The Satanic Bible* suggests the use of any drink that is stimulating and pleasing to the palate. Other things may be used by various groups.
8. Sword—The sword is a symbol of aggressive force. A knife (athame) can be used in place of it for private rituals.
9. Phallus—Used only in organized group rituals, any phallic symbol that can sprinkle water will do.
10. Gong—A concert gong is considered best, but any gong with a good, rich sound will do.
11. Parchment—Requests for magical operations (blessings or curses, for instance) are written on a parchment which is then burned.

Other sources list five basic tools for witchcraft, which also may be used by Satanists:

1. The witch's knife, or athame.
2. The witch's cord, or girdle cord. This is a "rope" traditionally made from flax or river rushes and is approximately six feet long.
3. The witch's censer, or thurible. This is a bowl-shaped object used to burn incense or mix solutions.
4. The witch's cup, or chalice.
5. The grimoire, or Book of Shadows. The grimoire contains the spells compiled by an individual or group.

Indoor Satanic Ritual Site

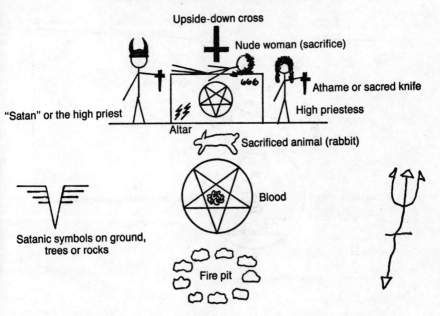

There would be a pentagram circle on the floor, an altar, candles (usually black, but they may be white or red), perhaps a skull, various symbols on walls and floor, an athame or witch's knife, swords, an upside-down cross on the wall, and lamps or candles set around on the floor. "Worshipers" wear robes until the signal is given for all to be naked. Animals sometimes are sacrificed and the blood splattered over the area and people. A woman may be used sexually on the altar by all men present. An orgy may follow.

Outdoor Satanic Ritual Site

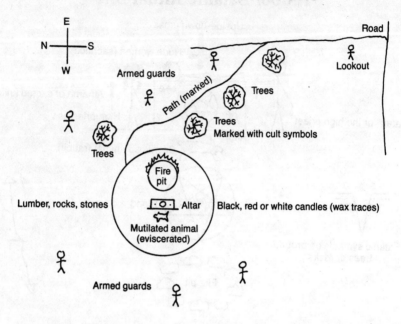

- There are always lookouts and guards, and they will be armed. There are two rings of guards; the inner ring will fight.
- Markings on trees warn others that this is a ritual spot. They announce to Satanists that the spot is near. Other signs on trees point the way (much like Boy Scout signs).
- Mutilated animals (dogs, cats, rabbits, squirrels, pigs, cows, horses, and/or their bones) may be found, plus dolls, knives, candles [or wax], lamps, robes.
- Any number from four or five to the traditional thirteen or several hundred cultists may gather for a

ritual. Sexual orgies may take place, especially in the form of the black mass.

- A magic circle may be traced in dirt or marked out with stones or candles. The rite is carried on inside the circle.

The Occult Holidays

Since ancient times, pagan and occult religions have observed certain holidays. The rituals and traditions of these holidays were designed to appease various gods, insure a good harvest, or work certain kinds of magic. The religious practices of modern witches as well as Satanists have their roots in these ancient beliefs.

Historically, worship of the moon (or a moon goddess) predates the worship of the sun (or sun god); therefore, the four major festivals of the various moon cults are the ones most commonly observed:

Halloween (*October 31*)—Halloween, or Samhain, marks the end of the growing season and harvest and the beginning of the destruction and death associated with winter. The power of the underworld is said to be unleashed, and the spirits are freed to travel about the earth. This would be considered an ideal time for contacting supposed spirits of the dead. Halloween is the end/beginning of the witches' year.

Candlemas (*February 2*)—Candlemas, the Feast of Saint Bride, or Brigid, marked the coming of spring, the growing length of days, and the end of the rule of death and destruction. Some moon cults celebrated the recovery of the moon goddess, after having given birth to the new sun god, six weeks before, on the shortest day of the year.

Beltane (April 30)—Also known as Walpurgisnacht or Roodmas, Beltane was for some a day to honor Saint Walburga (Walburg is also an old Teutonic name for the festival for the god of the underworld). It more or less coincides with the time of the year for planting, and the Celts offered human sacrifice at this time of year.

Lammas (July 31)—Lammas or Lugnasad roughly coincides with the beginning of the harvest season; fruits and vegetables would be ripening, and farmers would soon be bringing in crops. In some of the old religions the priest-king was sacrificed in the fields.

Sabbats or Celebrations

Satanists and witches celebrate eight major Sabbats during the year. Each one holds significance to them. In addition, Satanists hold a member's birth date in reverence. On these dates there should be a significant amount of activity.

February 2	Candlemas or Ormelc
March 21	Equinoxes (1)
April 30	May Eve or Beltane
June 22	Solstics (1)
August 1	August or Lammas
September 21	Equinoxes (2)

October 31	Halloween
December 22	Solstics (2)

The most significant of these Sabbats are (in order):

Halloween
May Eve
Summer Solstics
Winter Solstics

If bizarre rituals are to occur within organized satanic groups, they will most likely occur on or about one of these dates.

Contract or Pact With Satan

THIS IS A CONTRACT. THE SIGNING OF THIS CONTRACT WOULD MEAN THE FOLLOWING:

1. That you worship and follow Satan.
2. That you will serve him and live in his name.
3. That you have broken, or will break all of the Ten Commandments.
4. That the breaking of the commandments will be, or was, in the name of Satan.
5. That you will not revert to being a Christ-loving fool. Yet if you decide to terminate your loyalty to Satan, you will remain neutral until the day of your death.
6. That after the decision of leaving Satan, and you have remained neutral, you will still receive the placement in hell, earned during your faithfulness to him, when you die.

7. That you will be treated equally like other members.
8. That you will participate in the cult's rituals (as often as possible).
9. That you will turn to a fellow member in times of grief and anger before acting rationally as far as suicide, terminating loyalty, etc.
10. That you will not discuss any of the cult's actions with anyone outside the cult.

If you have any questions about the above or of the cult, feel free to talk to the leader of the cult. Sign below if you agree with this contract. Note! You are not signing your soul to Satan by signing this contract.

Applicant's Signature: _____

Applicant's Age and Birthdate: _____

Date of Agreement: _____

Thank you!
Sinbad the Satanic Priest

(This contract was confiscated from a middle-school student.)

Using the Toys of the Damned

For the most part, the black mass of Louis XIV's time is not celebrated in contemporary Satanism. The exception would be the rather cleaned-up, legal rituals of the Church of Satan. In general, Satanism is much less liturgically correct than LaVey's church and less inclined to parody Christian ritual. The black occult is much more interested in the performance of "magic" (seeking power) or in glorifying the devil than it is in mocking Christ. Indeed, there are both "theistic" and "atheistic" Satanists; that is, some black occultists really do believe in the "existence" of Satan, while many others do not believe in the literal reality of Satan or of God. Many Satanists believe only in themselves; they think of themselves as "the devil"; they are their own "god."

In general, satanic worship is found in the fully developed sense only in the institutional or religious variety (Church of Satan; Temple of Set; Brotherhood of the Trapezoid) or in the underground, criminal Satanic cults. Among self-styled or teenage Satanists, the liturgies used are generally eclectically devised rites, based on LaVey's *The Satanic Bible*[1] and *The Satanic Rituals*.[2]

In almost every case, satanic rituals are done without slaughter of any kind, but some rites call for the killing of animals, and in these, German shepherds (or other large dogs) are the preferred victims. Teenage Satanists are apt to utilize neighborhood cats, small dogs, rabbits, and squirrels. I have knowledge of one ritual site where the mutilated body of a pig was found. In Louisiana and Oklahoma the carcasses of cows have been found, with the evidence of ritual mutilation. One site of such mutilation was behind the Indian school on the Fort Sill military reservation. During a lecture visit, I discussed this incident with the sheriff there. Maury Terry reports the discovery of dozens of carcasses of large dogs sacrificed in a park in Queens, New York.[3]

Not all satanic rites involve the death of animals. Perhaps most involve the sacrifice of pain by the persons involved. (*See* the reports on teenage satanism in chapter 1.) Satanists are prone to offer Satan themselves, through slashing themselves with razors or sharp knives, generally on the arms (usually the tops of the forearms, to avoid striking an artery), the upper sides of the thighs, or the buttocks. Shallow slashes across the chest or breasts are not unknown, but care is taken not to cause dangerous bleeding; this rite aims not so much at shedding blood but at causing pain. Some criminally involved Satanists, under the influence of alcohol and drugs, have reportedly cut off the joints of their fingers. The cultist starts with the first joint of the little finger at the first ritual and goes on to the second joint of the same finger at the next one. Satanists seek mutilation as an in-group sign, like tattoos in some cultures; but pain offered to Satan is the overarching point of this terrible practice.

Some satanic rites involve sexuality, much like the magical rites performed by Aleister Crowley. Sex is used to raise power; to demonstrate loyalty to Satan; and very often, to denigrate, to violate the innocence of someone. Although seduction by way of drug intoxication may be used on some women involved, many participate willingly. Satanic cults' abuse of women is similar to the abasement of the women who attach themselves to motorcycle gangs, because both appear to involve a kind of sadistic, masochistic relationship.

The imbibing of alcohol and the use of drugs of all kinds play a role in almost all satanic ritual, of whatever kind, from the self-styled Satanist to the criminal cults. Someone has observed that all such demonic liturgies are done by intoxicated participants.

Far too often persons connect human sacrifice with satanic rituals, and without doubt, such sacrifices are theoretically part of some specialized rites. However, apart from murder cases such as those discussed in chapter 1, little concrete proof exists of frequent ritual human sacrifice. The self-styled Satanists on Long Island did take a young man's life. Beyond all question, Constanzo led his occult group in at least twenty-three murders in Mexico City and in Matamoros, Mexico (while all these deaths may not have been parts of rituals, many were, including the death of Mark Kilroy).

Nonetheless, we need not become carried away by the many rumors and reports of human sacrifices that students in this field of study encounter, for they generally lack evidence. While it is certainly possible that criminal cults have performed human sacrifices on drifters, hitch-hikers, street people (the homeless), and recently born infants whose births are unrecorded, we cannot prove anything from silence. Unsuccessful attempts to find the remains of such victims have been made, as in a case in northwest Ohio, in the summer of 1985. Authorities dug up a field but found no bodies. In 1989, a yard was dug up in a small Oregon town, during the trial of several men accused of satanic activity. Nothing was found.

Some experts on occult behavior hold that criminal Satanists utilize crematoria to destroy all evidence or bury the remains under the casket in a recently dug grave. Though some claim that body parts washed up by the tide are the remains of satanic victims, generally authorities can trace these remains to "ordinary" murders (especially among drug dealers). Probably, therefore, human sacrifice forms little to no part of most satanic rituals. When it does occur, drug-intoxicated self-styled Satanists or criminal occultic groups enact the crime. (*See* chapter 7 for a discussion of satanic crime.)

We've come a long way since the amatory masses of the

fifteenth to the seventeenth century or the masses for inducing the death of someone in the seventh century. Now, satanic worship focuses more on the doing of evil, yet it has become more diffuse, as it embraces all ages and all segments of society. Outside the theaterlike presentations of the Church of Satan, satanic ritual today does not have the inverted Catholic mass as its model. The evil operates just as fully, but the form and texture of contemporary rites have declined.

7
Ritualized Crime:
The Trivialization of Moral Values

At the end of the twentieth century, the mere idea of a human being torturing and killing another person for a magical purpose seems absurd. Understandably many people, including some in law enforcement, will argue that such ritualized crime does not occur. Nonetheless, despite some doubtless exaggerations and false reports, hard physical evidence demonstrates the reality of ritual crime. The murders committed by Ricky Kasso, Jimmy Troiano, Jonathan Cantero, Tommy Sullivan, Sean Sellers, and the Matamoros cult, all discussed in chapter 1, along with other incidents not discussed here, prove it. No matter the denials and unwillingness to look and listen; no matter the cynical mockery made of those who do "look and see" and take such events seriously, we can connect ritualized crime with Satanism in North America.

For a long time criminologists have known about individuals who engage in ritual crime. Some, who have warped minds, become serial killers, acting out rituals that soon become evident to homicide investigators. True crime stories and movies, ranging from Jack the Ripper, in the nineteenth century, to Richard Ramirez, only recently found guilty of multiple murders in California, have made the ritual killer familiar to the public. In most cases, a twisted scenario of sexuality and violence seems to drive the killer. Often, as in the Green River slayings in the Pacific Northwest, these crimes remain almost impossible to solve beyond a reasonable doubt. Authorities who have studied serial killers observe that such people seem to kill simply because it makes them feel good. Sociopathic and sexually sadistic, some serial killers begin a long history of torture murders because it gives them a sense of power and a feeling of control.

These feelings of power, the desire to control, and the pathological pleasure in hurting others are emotions quite close to those expressed in the utter hedonism, the conscienceless pleasure seeking of the committed destructive occultist.

The Crimes of Satan?

For some years reports and some actual physical evidence has built up that tends to indicate an underground slaughter of small children. In March, 1986, the body of a day-old child was found near a trash barrel at Mohegan Park, in Fairfield, Connecticut. This white male child had been suffocated and his head and face disfigured. Coins, food, and trinkets indicative of one of the Afro-Caribbean cults were left with the body.[1]

In the same year a deputy in a rural Oregon sheriff's department found the dismembered parts of a newborn girl's body inside a garbage bag thrown into a dumpster. The investigator felt a satanic ritual might have been responsible for this murder, since the head was removed cleanly, the body was drained of blood, and the arms were elongated, possibly indicating that it was hung upside down to drain it of blood. The time of death was near or on April 30, Walpurgisnacht, the second most important holiday in the satanic calendar.[2]

Some defectors from satanic cults, chiefly young women, report that such groups use newborn infants, born out of wedlock, at home, to cult members. The births of such babies are said not to be reported or recorded. This horrible scenario suggests that a supply of ritual victims, who legally do not exist, might be available for sadistic satanic rituals.[3] Of course, no one can prove such an allegation without evidence, but the discovery of the bodies of newborns, like those mentioned above, may support it. Such gruesome finds are made from time to time around the country, but investigators have a problem separating cases of child murder per se or child abandonment from ritualized murder. Only when occult materials appear with the body, as in the Connecticut case, can we clearly identify it as a satanic crime.

Maury Terry maintains that many serial killers are adherents of destructive occultism or are out-and-out Satanists.[4] This may hold true in some instances—certainly Richard Ramirez shows something of the "satanic syndrome," and perhaps David Berkowitz, the infamous "Son of Sam," harbored occult beliefs—but it is difficult to accept Terry's hypothesis. Conspiracy theories—and Terry does offer a "loose" satanic-conspiracy theory—rarely turn out to be true. Again, there have always been serial killers, and while they may exhibit some common traits (as defined in the FBI serial-murderer profile), they also show many dissimilarities. Probably mental disorders account for the tendency towards multiple or mass murders more than adherence to any ideology such as occultism.[5]

One needs to make only careful general statements about the psychopathology of any one or any class of persons, including those involved in the black occult, in Satanism of whatever type, or in criminality per se. No satisfactory evidence exists about the extent to which mental illness or emotional disturbance accounts for in the commission of a crime. We can only say that about a quarter of those incarcerated show signs of psychotic, neurotic, or emotional disturbance. But we may safely generalize that personality traits and behaviors favoring criminality do not have to involve overt psychoses or serious neuroses. Strong emotional disturbances in the "right" situation and time may impel the person to overt criminal behavior. Someone with the wrong attitude, in the wrong place, at the wrong time may well take criminal action, yet those chance events defy prediction. Once a person has taken a criminal course, however, strong evidence exists that he or she will repeat a specific type of crime, unless intervention and incarceration prevent it. The serial murderer, who generally has no connection with his victim, frequently escapes detection after his first murder. He then is likely to commit a similar crime when the attitude (hostility, sexual frustration, or whatever), the situation (a lonely place, the presence of a weaker person), and the time (near an anniversary, the full moon, and so forth) are similar to the first murder. Unless the police intervene or a victim kills or injures the attacker or at least survives and identifies the perpetrator, the killer will go on and on, from situation to situation, becoming a serial murderer.

In a word, serial killers are loners, eccentric and perverse. They are not "joiners." Such psychopaths or sociopaths are content with their own interior, private, solitary fantasy life. When such a person invites someone else into his private "ritual," it is to kill that person as part of it.

Although Satanists are sadistic, they probably have a different mental and emotional profile from the actual serial killer. This is not to say that some Satanists may not devolve into multiple killers or that a solitary, self-styled Satanist may not be a serial murderer. Some serial killers quite likely were solitary black occultists or degenerated cultic Satanists, but this does not mean that all—or even most—serial killers are into occultism. Satanism is a social and individual pathology, but other social and personal pathologies exist, as they always have.

Nonetheless, the occult pretensions of multiple murderers Charles Manson and Richard Ramirez and the proven ritual sacrifices in Matamoros by Adolfo de Jesus Constanzo illustrate the potential for mass murder that lurks in the subculture of black occultism. The craziness induced by drug intoxication among alienated people (the very kind drawn to the black occult), with its attendant paranoia and hostility, make the possibility of mass violence by cultic Satanists even greater. There are other forms of mayhem than the scenario of the serial killer.

The Trivialization of Humanity

Slaughter by either self-styled Satanists, cultic or criminal Satanists, or by other types of serial killers demonstrates the trivialization of human life that inevitably follows the trivialization of human values. To those who have no empathy with others, the lives of others have no worth. Such a psychopath can take another's life without a crisis of conscience. To him, other persons are simply things to be used, tools to relieve tension, frustration, or sexual pressure. The ritualistic aspect of many serial killings, which involve inhuman tortures and mutilations after death, shows the killers' evaluation of other persons as worthless, except for the role the victims can play in their private fantasies. One might speak of a transvaluation of all values, in the terms of the mentally degenerating Friedrich Nietzsche, in which the value of the other person, for the pathological personality, becomes that of an object in their imaginary world.

Such a transvaluation is also true of extreme hedonists such as Satanists. In several cases of murder by teenage or self-styled Satanists, they explained their actions by saying they killed to see what the experience was like. The sense of power, of utter control over someone's life or death, has greater value to such killers than the victim's life. The selfish search for pleasure encouraged in Satanism of all types builds a gateway to immoral behavior like this. Ultimately, such trivialization of the worth of others leads to a sense of one's own worthlessness, to a painful sense of meaninglessness. All that remains is the pursuit of physical pleasure, until that becomes possible only under intense stimulation. At that point, the abuse of others sadistically, or the masochistic abuse of one's own body may begin.

Children in Destructive Occultism

Nothing has caused more media sensationalism than the many reports of child abuse connected to Satanism. Two of these involved army posts, West Point and the Presidio, in San Francisco. The most notorious case was the McMartin Day Care Center, in Manhattan Beach, California.

Satanism has been receiving an increasing amount of media attention all over the United States as an apparent motive for criminal activity, ranging from vandalism and animal mutilation to kidnapping, child abuse, and murder. The cases in the news are isolated, but there are indications that these are only the tip of the iceberg.

Victims of occult child abuse tend to tell the same kinds of stories: of being forced to drink blood and/or eat flesh, of being molested by adults—who are sometimes masked or robed—as part of a kind of ceremony. Present at the scene or in the children's descriptions are common satanic symbols such as the inverted pentagram, the upside-down cross, and the like. Many of these child-abuse cases are not provable, due to factors such as the age of the child, the child's inability to understand what has taken place, and often the reluctance of adults—both parents and investigators—to consider the possibility of such a thing. Besides these, other cases in Minnesota and Nevada have drawn much attention. The Minneapolis, Minnesota, case ultimately proved to have no foundation, and in the McMartin case, only a few of many original defendants ended up on trial. All defendants were found not guilty, although one was arraigned on other charges. Many public officials have discounted the satanic element in all of these cases.

Others, such as occult investigator and former FBI special agent in charge Ted Gundersen, allege that the satanic involvement first reported in these cases is real. Since the witnesses in these cases are very small children, it is indeed difficult to ascertain the facts. Some psychologists and prosecutors see these child victims as further victims who have the satanic element of their stories suggested to them by hysterical adults. Other competent persons believe these children have been systematically abused in occult ritualistic settings. Disentangling the truth from fiction proves difficult, if not impossible.

Parents have reported other cases in which their children have been victimized in satanic rituals. Most of these—and I have had a score or more reported to me, from across the nation—involve separated parents. Usually it is the father who practices Satanism. The mother reports that the father takes the children to satanic rituals, where they are sexually abused, during the time the divorced father has visiting rights or custody of the children. Once more, because such charges come in the midst of child-custody conflict, it is difficult to find the truth.

Even more horrifying are the reports from women (or their counselors) who claim satanic groups have used them as "breeders." Breeders are said to be those chosen to be impregnated at cult orgies so that they may bear the babies to be used as sacrifices on the high holidays of the satanic calendar. Many of these women are now diagnosed as having MPD (multiple personality disorder) or else as having PTS (posttraumatic stress syndrome). I have had a half dozen or more such cases reported to me either by the women themselves or by their psychologists or psychiatrists. Some counselors claim that there has been an upsurge in the number of MPD cases diagnosed in the last decade.

The stories told by these claimed breeders are truly horrible. Each speaks of ritual rape, of seclusion during pregnancy, of bearing the child at home, and of seeing the child killed or killing the child herself at a satanic ceremony. The body is then said to be cannibalized for blood and organs and bones used in black magic and the rest burned. Even more terrible, many of the women said they repeated these pregnancies many times. The satanic holidays need human sacrifices, and "breeding" is the surest, safest way to guarantee a steady supply, these women claim.

Without exception, the breeders who have told me these stories say that such events happened years ago. They also claim to have repressed these memories for a long time, although they have recently begun to surface in dreams or in the free association of psychotherapy. Most such women declared that nightmares brought this material to their attention, but they didn't understand what the dreams meant until they entered psychotherapy. Oftentimes, the counselor first contacted me to inquire about the meaning of symbols or the structure of a ritual that had surfaced in the patient's dreams or free associations. No one could provide physical evidence to verify these claims. To my knowledge—and I questioned patients and counselors carefully on this—the patient gave no details as to place, time, and persons present, which could be checked. I must be fair and say that I am not convinced of the truth of such claims, and I find such an increase in cases of MPD incredible. After much thought, I believe that the claims of breeders and great numbers of MPD cases are classic examples of urban legends. The reality of satanic crime makes unthinking belief in unsupported claims unnecessary. I may be wrong, of course, but logically there is no cause to accept claims without proof. Additionally, the undisputed influence of *Michelle Remembers,* an unsubstantiated story of a woman who "remembers" being satanically abused as a child,[6] on all subsequent breeder stories renders all such reports suspect. The psychiatrist in British Columbia who wrote *Michelle Remembers* offered no physical or documentary proof of "Michelle's" claims. So far, no other breeder has shown proof either. Let the reader make up his or her own mind.

The Great However

However, a close parallel exists between the abuse of children reportedly done by Satanists and the proven child abuse of several new religions or "cults." Court cases have decided that child abuse did take place in several black religious cults derived from fundamentalism. In such groups, *discipline* is often a code word for "sadistic mistreatment of little children." The worst cases of child sexual abuse surfaced in the sixties-era cult the Children of God, now called the Family of Love.[7] I helped Una McManus, for five years a COG member, tell her story in *Not for a Million Dollars.* Una left the group because she feared for the safety of her two young sons. Moses David (or David Brandt Berg), the cult leader, introduced "Flirty Fishing," or prostitution, to attract followers and earn money by female members, then expanded such "hooking for Jesus" to men in the group. He also advocated child sex, encouraging parents to masturbate their children and to have sex with them. Berg did all this while claiming to head a fundamentalist Christian group! It is hard to see how the Children of God could be differentiated from a satanic cult insofar as this behavior is concerned.

On the basis of the actual abuse we know took place and still takes place in certain of the new religions (which I have called "destructive cults"[8]), it is not difficult to believe that such child abuse takes place in underground or criminal satanic cults. After all, if such horrors can arise in groups supposedly based on the Bible, what can we reasonably expect from groups based on selfish, hedonistic power and pleasure seeking? The only question is just how far does the abuse of children go in destructive occultism? No one can as yet give a definitive answer, but some of us are trying to uncover the facts needed to formulate the answer.

8
Challenging Satan's Realm

Recently, a coroner in Kentucky spoke of a strange case he investigated in 1980.[1] His area is sparsely populated: a land of hills and trees, with low land prices. During the 1970s, the San Francisco and New York "underground" newspapers advertised cheap acreage here. Many offbeat groups and back-to-the-land hippie communes bought land and migrated to Kentucky. My friend said some of these new folks were fine people. Gradually, the tents and old schoolhouses, and even caves, that they first lived in gave way to modest homes. The one-time settlers now work as mechanics, teachers, and even in county jobs. But a few were stranger than anyone could guess. One man had all his teeth pulled, except for the canine teeth; these he had sharpened into fangs. He dressed in black, wore a black cape, and slept in a coffin. In every way possible, he tried to be a vampire.

One day a passing motorist spotted something strange in a roadside dump near the "vampire's" hovel—the skull of a child. The motorist took it to the coroner, who began a seventy-five-man search of the area. Some posse members uncovered a child's vertebrae in a fire site, directly in front of the "vampire's" cabin. By this time, the occultist had fled. Believing a murder had taken place, the authorities put out an all-points bulletin for the "vampire." After some weeks he was apprehended in Woodstock, Illinois. This strange person attracted police attention by leaping out of the shadows at people on the street. He would bare his "fangs" and furl his cape. When arrested, the "vampire" was sleeping in a coffin.

Medical examination of the skull showed that it was not a murder victim's but that of a corpse stolen from a cemetery in Woodstock. The only charge that could be brought in Kentucky was one of illegal cremation. Of course, grave-robbery charges were brought in Illinois.

As pathetic, even silly as this account is, it does show something of the occult underground world. Those fascinated by the occult and drawn to the practices of Satanism are obsessed with the dark, the filthy, the dead, the irreverent, and the antisocial. My investigation of a satanic coven twenty years ago, in a larger city, uncovered a brisk underground economy: a trade in skulls, bones, and body parts stolen from graves in another state. Most of us enjoy the fun of children at Halloween, but clearly such a fascination with dead bodies is a sign of emotional, if not mental, illness.

Almost ten years later, in March, 1989, just across the hill in this remote area of Kentucky, a mysterious, as-yet-unexplained death occurred. This victim was totally devoted to ingesting psychedelic mushrooms, and the materials and tools needed to cultivate the mushrooms and marijuana covered his property. When a youth brought a deputy sheriff out to check on a "sick man," the deputy found the victim sitting up, dead, without a mark of distress. Tests by the state pathologist have yet to show a cause of death.

Even more strangely, while the deputy was inspecting the body, a number of cars drove into this truly out-of-the-way, back-of-beyond spot. Fifteen persons, dressed in black robes, got out and began to chant. More cars were arriving when the solitary deputy became concerned and forced the crowd off the property at gunpoint. The coroner of Metcalfe County, Kentucky, where this event took place, called me to assist in the investigation in April, 1989. As late as May, 1990, we were still working on this baffling happening.

Some historians understand medieval witchcraft as a political movement or, in our terms, as a protest movement. They say a small number of serfs, oppressed by the lords, landowners, and clergy, turned to midnight prayers to Satan. These serfs saw God as an oppressor, since their unsympathetic leaders claimed that God had established the feudal order that enslaved them. Not receiving what they prayed for in church made these people believe that Satan, God's enemy, might be more understanding. Perhaps, the reasoning of such historians goes, if the serf gave his loyalty to the devil (as to a feudal lord), then Satan would protect and prosper him. In that light, evil became the occultist's good.

The Hedonistic Revolt

Unlike the serfs, modern Satanists generally have no political ax to grind, but they, too, revolt against society.

Since at least the 1960s, the spirit of American culture has been one of an unbridled search for pleasure. Satanism takes unbounded physical pleasure to its ultimate lengths. The entryway into the broad path of occult destruction leads through promiscuous sexual behavior—both straight and gay—overconsumption of alcohol, and drug abuse.

The Matamoros drug-smuggling cult of Adolfo de Jesus Constanzo amply illustrates the connection between homosexuality and drug use and destructive occultism. Constanzo's group has received little continuing follow-up, except, for the wrong reasons, in "trash" media. This is a shame, for the uncovering of the Matamoros tragedy evidences the real demonic underground of destructive occultism that does exist, despite the effects of such journalism to exploit and to trivialize it.

To embrace the antithetical, the contrapuntal, the opposite, to wish for the triumph of chaos over order means becoming a moral invert. That is the Satanic choice. The Satanist chooses death over life, darkness over light. He seeks not to be immoral but amoral, a position which he shares with millions of amoral, relativistic persons in North America.

Even among non-Satanists, a supposed Christian often embraces moral relativity; no wonder, then, so many count fornication, drunkenness, adultery and drug-induced escapism as good, for all these perversions of goodness have the short-term result of making one physically "feel good." No matter that, as John Stuart Mill declared in the controversy over utilitarianism, with Jeremy Bentham, all pleasure cannot be considered equal, for that would make the life of a pig equal to that of a man.[2]

Any person who embraces the quest for pleasure with

the principle, "If it makes me feel good or feel good about myself, I'll do it," has elected to be a pig, not a person. Even more, such a person elects to become a pig through the possibilities of degradation that are open only to human beings. So many in our society engage in life-destroying behavior like alcohol and drug abuse and promiscuous sexuality, with its high degree of risk for sexually transmitted diseases, including AIDS. Middle-class teenagers reared as hedonists often end as suicide statistics, because the life of a pig cannot ultimately satisfy a human being. Yet many people today seem interested in "pigging out" on every physical pleasure and emotional experience possible.

Finally, such amoral materialism, seen in the world of religion (consider the Jim and Tammy Bakker scandal at PTL Ministries, the hypocrisy of Jimmy Swaggart, and the bizarre and irreverent money-making scheme of Oral Roberts); in politics (payoffs and sex scandals); in government (the resignations of Spiro Agnew and Richard Nixon) and in the university (the basketball scandals at the University of Kentucky), is the real cause for the rise of destructive occultism. Hypocrisy is the tribute that vice pays to virtue. Satanism is unconcerned with the appearances of things. The black occultist knows that the values of our society have changed, and he welcomes the change. Recognizing the evil that all of us have created in God's good world, the client of the devil has decided that the evil all around us is more desirable than the good that created and sustains the universe.

The Ultimately Radical Departure

As these stories and cultural truths testify, Satanism is about the irrational, the bizarre, and the weird; so it probably will not seem any more logical and understandable once I have rationalized the behavior of some American young—and older—people. We can describe irrational behavior; we can point to bizarre events; we can theorize about the internal events of people caught up in emotional illness or occult behaviors. But we can, finally, only intuit, only feel with them sympathetically, because their thoughts and actions are off the scale of rational, linear thought.

Involvement in alternative religious groups and in the occult represents a "radical departure," in the words of medical doctor Saul Levine, from the social world of middle-class America.[3] It is a rebellious act on the part of teenagers, an act of separation (and thus at least an attempt at claiming adult responsibility over their lives), from parents, family, church, school, and community environment.

SOME COMMON SIGNS OF SATANIC PRACTICES

A TYPICAL PROFILE
Intelligent.
Creative.
Curious.
Possibly an underachiever.
Usually male.
Middle- or upper-middle-class
  family.
Low self-esteem.
Difficulty relating to peers.

Alienation from family religion.

Stress with accompanying anxiety and fear.

Feelings of inadequacy or loss of control.

Obsession with fantasy role-playing games.

Obsession with heavy-metal rock music.

Books on magic, witchcraft, paganism, Satanism, grimoires (personal Book of Shadows).

Objects used for spells or rituals: candles (tapered or in the form of a human figure), candle holders, incense, knives, inverted pentagram or inverted cross, and the number 666.

Symbolic jewelry.

Drug use—incense is a common cover-up for the odor of some drugs.

Unexplained paranoia or fear of the world.

Extremely secretive. The child will begin stashing things away and will refuse to talk about anything that relates to his or her involvement. If the subject of Satanism is brought up by a parent, for example, the child is likely to be unresponsive.

Fear of discussing involvement
due to belief that others in the
group will know, physically or
otherwise, that something has
been said.

This separation or rebellion may vary from a mild self-assertion to a violent confrontation, depending upon the degree of hostility in the young person. Hostility largely stems from frustration; overneglect; boredom; lack of meaningful discipline and communication; loss of impulse control due to drug or alcohol abuse, which often results from previous frustration; or out of feelings of guilt, shame, self-contempt, and lack of self-worth. The minimal attention the young person receives has become a built-in feature of much American life, because both parents work outside the home or are heavily involved in social lives of their own. This may form the basis for such ego deprivation or lack of self-esteem.

Some radical and destructive behavior is based on a simple play to get (at last) some personal attention, but it is too simplistic to put all such behavior down to ego aggrandizement.

In all events, dissatisfaction, ranging from boredom to the violently hostile, exists in all young people who break with their families and look for other authority figures, attention, and ego support in alternative social groups. In general, the more hostility (that is, psychic pain) in a youth, the more radically bizarre the behavior and/or belief system he or she will embrace. Satanism represents the ultimately radical break with middle-class society, whether or not the family is religious.

In all radical breaks, youths seem to seek:

1. *A source of power and authority in their lives.* This is why most cult leaders are dominant, chauvinistic older men or, in a smaller way, strong, powerful women.
2. *An escape from the routine.* Such youths desire a call to adventure and experience a fascination with the novel, in their efforts to combat boredom.
3. *A source of personal attention and a feeling of importance.* This may take the form of praise or blame.
4. *An ally who gives voice and action to the perceived failure and feelings of dissatisfaction felt in the home, church, school, and community.*

This leads to:

1. Allegiance to a strong cult (or occultic) leader—father, or mother, or master. The leader may derive authority from: God, as in the case of the Reverend Sun Myung Moon (The Unification Church) or Moses David (the Children of God or Family of Love); experience (such as supposed training in India or Tibet, or meditation or astral-travel experiences, as in the case of L. Ron Hubbard [Scientology] or Paul Twitchell [Eckankar] or in groups like Silva Mind Control or Transcendental Meditation); or initiation in occult knowledge, such as in wicca or witchcraft, forms of theosophy, neopaganism, ceremonial "magic," or Satanism (Anton LaVey; Colonel Michael Aquino).

   This relationship, of child to father or student to teacher, is traditional and thus satisfying to the young.

2. Consequently only offbeat, unusual teachings—against the prevailing norms—satisfy the rebelling young person. The more different, the stronger the attraction.

3. The youth gains personal attention, both positive and negative, as he or she struggles to master a new set of teachings and to learn to practice new disciplines (behaviors).

4. The leader, group, and teachings thus legitimate and give powerful voice to the dissatisfactions felt by the youth in rebellion.

5. The young person also receives a strong feeling of belonging, of solidarity, of "family," from the new group. Loneliness disappears. Even to be punished for infractions means that one is being taken seriously. Obviously this need is a reaction to the many broken marriages in America.

6. He or she receives a strong sense of self-worth, of importance, and thus of power as a member of a disciplined "in" group.

7. This new position can release the feelings of sacrifice, of contributions to important goals, as well as of self-aggrandizement, of reward for commitment and hard work. "Moonies" and Satanists seem to me to be on opposite ends of the spectrum here, as Moonies are generally hard working and self-sacrificing, while Satanists are concerned only for their physical pleasure.

8. As part of a group the young person may feel a sense of financial security; indeed, in cases of cultic Satanism, all participants may become involved in drug distribution. Selling drugs may give the young person money as well as personal access to drugs and

alcohol and free sexual favors. This "feedback" may reinforce the loyalty of the young person to the group.

Two types of students seem most susceptible to the lure of the black occult: The first type (which often produces a self-styled Satanist leader) is a bit discouraging, since in many ways it represents the intellectual elite of our high-school students; the second consists of those whom teachers, counselors and parents would expect to be involved in antisocial activity—marginal students who are already behavior problems because of bad home backgrounds and/or abuse of alcohol and/or drugs.

The first type, the bright, curious student, becomes fascinated by the intricacies of ceremonial magic and the rituals of the occult. Today this may include a passion for psychic phenomena—ESP, astral projection, reincarnation, regression, hypnosis, and the like. Such an intellectual may form a one-person cult or become the focus and leader of a small coven or group in the high school. (Often this is how a bookish student competes with his more athletic peers.)

The second type is the behavior problem looking for a place to act out hostilities and frustrations and to gain some sense of superiority by belonging to a secret, elite group. This may include the bully who finds ego support in extracting fear from other students. In fact, fear among students forms the primary evidence of the existence of such groups, and spreading fear may become a satanic group's primary goal. Young people with low self-esteem experience a lot of hostility, which appears in the form of sadism, and a lot of jealousy. (Sadomasochism is an important dynamic in satanic groups.)

Dealing With Destructive Occultism

Anyone who wishes to help a young person involved in Satanism must know that no magical answers, no quick solutions work. "Pop psychology" or "deliverance sermons" won't solve the problem. Involvement in Satanism is symptomatic of underlying problems, rather than the problem itself. For some youths, joining the "bad guys" may be a cry for help with the overwhelming problems; they act out offbeat behavior as an attention-getting device.

The Bible recognizes that involvement with demons grows from a vacuum, an unmet need or needs in a person's life. We can learn from Jesus' parable of the man exorcised of a demon:

> "When the unclean spirit has gone out of a man, he passes through waterless places seeking rest; and finding none he says, 'I will return to my house from which I came.' And when he comes he finds it swept and put in order. Then he goes and brings seven other spirits more evil than himself, and they enter and dwell there; and the last state of that man becomes worse than the first."
>
> Luke 11:24–26

In other words you can take a youth out of a satanic group and cut him off from occult literature and influence and not really deal with the problems. In a short time the spiritual and emotional vacuum within the young person will pull him into some other form of destructive behavior.

Therefore, I can offer only hard advice that will cost time, energy, and money to put into practice:

1. In the case of a youth only marginally involved or attracted or frightened by a satanic group, advise him to run, to "just say no" (as Mrs. Reagan said about drugs), to get away, and to keep away from those heavily involved. This single piece of advice will work for some.

2. In the case of a youth starved for personal attention, give him his due. Attention must be paid to every human being. Try to support his ego, to strengthen his self-esteem by your positive regard—and time—as a parent, teacher, counselor, or clergy. "Quality time" means rationed time. Such a youth needs *quantity* time.

3. In both the above cases, and in the residual, hard-core cases, attempt to introduce a youth to a positive influence, a constructive philosophy that will fill the emptiness in his or her life—especially concerning a value system.

4. Of course, if a youth has alcohol or drug-abuse problems, care and treatment for that must begin. Occult involvement and drug abuse are often symbiotic; they grow and flourish together. Remove one part of the system, and the other may die—unless a deep psychological or physiological dependence on alcohol or drugs has already developed.

5. Remember, occultism is essentially irrational, so you won't be likely to rationally argue someone out of belief in it. People do not become involved in occultism for logical reasons but emotional or spiritual ones. Therefore, the treatment must focus on care and healing of the emotions

and a deepening and redirection of the youth's spiritual interests. A long-standing truth in religious counseling and pastoral care says that there is nothing more life changing than the expulsive power of a new affection. To turn off one harmful belief system, turn on a constructive, satisfying belief system. This is the real power behind genuine conversions.

6. In a pluralistic society this does not mean, and cannot mean, that all court authorities, counselors, schoolteachers, and administrators can do is to hold a Christian revival! For every person that might help, it would raise problems for someone else. We must respect religious freedom in America, including the freedom of people not to adhere to a religion. Many of us wish we could offer a biblical alternative to everyone, and we can and do offer that in our churches and their outreach programs. In secular forums such as professional meetings, the schools, and other governmental functions, because of our American separation of church and state, we must respond sensitively to the choices of others. I and others who speak to such audiences experience the frustration of this dichotomy, but as Christians, we do not want to take advantage of our fellow citizens. We are here to help, not to dominate.

7. Therefore efforts to fill the spiritual and emotional vacuum in a troubled youth must take into account the youth's family's traditions and beliefs and fully respect the young person's rights. If this means exposure to an ethical philosophy or to some secular expression of values, rights, and obligations, we may have to live with that.

However counselors and family *cannot* neglect the need to confront the youth with some value system that respects one's own life and the lives, rights, and property of other people. The need to teach respect for oneself and for others is imperative.

When a counselor utilizes the troubled youth's family religion, he or she can confidently state that all the various communions of Christianity, Judaism, Islam, and of Buddhism, Hinduism, and other traditional faiths teach precisely such self-respect and respect for others. In some form, the Golden Rule appears in every faith. Sanctions against harming self and others, against stealing, lying, permissive sexuality, and hostility are taught by every religion.

Consequently, if the counselor can put the youth into meaningful touch with his family's religious tradition, that may greatly speed the removal of the emotional impasse and the filling of the spiritual vacuum.

8. Where, as is often the case today, no immediate family religious tradition exists, an attempt must be made to introduce the youth to an ethical philosophy, a system of values that broadens the youth's empathy with others and concern for them, while also introducing him to the concept of limitations on behavior, impulse control, and self-restraint. *Freedom* does not mean "license to say and do anything we think we want to say or do"; it means we operate within the boundaries of our own, self-chosen restraints. After all, whether or not they realize it, in order to live in harmony, people must have a social contract that allows each one a place in the world. Indeed, some youth involved in destructive behavior appear to need socialization.

9. Overall, counselors of such youth will need tough love, a personal concern enclosed in firmness. Behavior

problems among youth are the external signs of a lack of internalized discipline or self-discipline. Some have suggested that first offenders in the criminal justice system be offered the chance at shorter sentences if they volunteer for a military style boot-camp experience. For some youth, this type of conditioning may be beneficial. But they do not need brutality, with authority figures who use sheer force to make the youth obey; the young people need to be challenged and helped to succeed in something, whether they drill with a pine log or swim with a full pack or make a rose garden. They must achieve a sense of competence and develop confidence in their interactions with others. People need to feel good about themselves, on the basis of having struggled to do something good or constructive. Merely telling people they are good—when in their hearts they believe they are not good—won't do it. These youth and all youth need affirmation, attention, praise for constructive behaviors, and caring, accepting criticism of negative behavior—not their personhood. This form of behaviorism builds up "conscience," an internal regulatory principle.

The young Satanist requires a rite of passage, a challenge, an adventure that will not destroy others and the community. Life is hard, but the young person needs to learn that with courage and work, he or she can be tough enough to live happily while enhancing others' happiness. Life is fragile and must be preserved. Life—that of others or our own—is precious; we must not waste it. The strong are happy—though these people do not necessarily have the most physical power—because they have spiritual strength. Those who find strength in achieving power over others by spreading fear portray their own inner weakness and fear. The Bible tells us ". . . perfect love casts out fear" (1 John 4:18)—a truth both religious and secular persons should accept.

By focusing the Satanist's attention on these truths, the counselor can provide an alternative to the hedonistic satanic philosophies. Because of the rebellion involved in occult involvement, the Satanist will initially abhor the idea of a parent, government, or God who might say no to any of his whims. However, under the black robe or behind the frightening tattoo, the destructive occultist is more like the rest of us than he—or we—can comfortably admit. All of us have trouble changing our course and saying no to worldly pleasure. The strength to do that can only come from the expulsive power of a new affection.

9
From Darkness to Light

Like the kinetic energy accumulated in an earth fault, the many forces in our mid-twentieth-century civilization seemed to build toward a major cultural earthquake. Marshal McLuhan spoke of the shift from hot to cool media of communication, from the linear logic of the printed book to the all-encompassing television "massage" of the human psyche. Paul Tillich preached about the shaking of the foundations of Western culture by the many philosophical, religious, and political developments of the nineteenth and early twentieth centuries. A group of younger, liberal theologians in the mid-1960s looked at the new life-styles and beliefs of Americans and proclaimed the death of God.

At the same time, the seemingly solid rock foundations of a way of life: white superiority, male control, the dominance of logic over passion and the invincibility of the United States' power were challenged and thrown into disarray by the civil rights movement, the rise of feminism, the glorification of "flower power," and the endless, frustrating war in Vietnam. By the mid-1970s the streets of America reflected new religious cults, from blue-suited, neatly clipped Moonies to head-shaved, white-robed, chanting Krishnas.

On the marquees of movie houses and the shelves of bookstores the half-gods of occultism announced themselves. The Age of Aquarius had gone mad. *Rosemary's Baby; The Omen*, and its many sequels; *Salem's Lot*, ad nauseum; along with *Nightmare on Elm Street* and its numerous follow-ups filled the need for entertainment once met by Humphrey Bogart, Gary Cooper, and Katherine Hepburn. A tortured, sweating exorcist replaced a tall, taciturn lawman as the object of all eyes. Many said people had trouble believing in the biblical God. Others, with more truth, observed that people had trouble accepting what the biblical God required in the way of human conduct. If God proscribed adultery or homosexuality, if he showed extramarital sex or drunkenness to be sinful, then God could simply go. But somehow, the need for the transcendent remained. God might have to go, but the lord of self-indulgence could very well stay. The half-god rose to power on a wave of popular sentiment which had made *vox populi* the *vox Dei*. A God who stood in the way of men and women's desires did not die, as radical theologians declared. Rather, God was banished, as the disciplined Socrates was offered banishment by the Athenians or as an overthrown king is driven away from his native land. In God's place, by the silent default of the majority and the active endorsement of the few, Satan took center stage.

The growth of destructive occultism took time. In fact, occultism in general, under the public-relations image of the New Age still works hard to consolidate its cultural position. Millions still feel God's continuing life and influence, although it sometimes seems many of his self-appointed defenders have done as much to damage his cause as have the occultists! The issue today is still in doubt.

How do God-fearing people fight Satanism in a society that emphasizes the personal pursuit of fleshly desires as the real meaning of freedom? Where the law protects deviancy, the theist, the Christian, must accept the challenge to instruct and persuade. We cannot take the supposed "easy route" of passing laws to suppress (but not really eradicate) the demonic in our midst. An attempt to use secular laws to put down unpopular expressions of "religion" not only contradicts our pluralistic government, it proves counterproductive on other fronts. More often than not, Christians who raise the flag of panic about the presence of destructive occultism find it backfires on them.

The church can take no shortcuts in its mission to fight Satan and evangelize all people. While existing laws may be—and ought to be—used to suppress demonstrated criminal acts and to protect persons threatened by destructive occultists, the occultists themselves, including Satanists, can be countered only by persuasion and the preaching of the Gospel. The church must come to see persons oppressed by the occult as the proper subject of special evangelistic attention.

Attempting to Convert the Occultist

Most of us professionally involved with social problems look a bit suspiciously at simple answers to complex problems. Even those of us committed to our religious faith may view dogmatic pronouncements about conversion as the answer to every problem skeptically. Conversion is a desirable goal, but most people do not reach it as clearly and swiftly as old-fashioned revivalism seemed to suggest. The move from alienated, drug-confused participation in destructive occultism to conversion seems straight and sure only when we look back upon it. Indeed, the sheer implausibility of such a change of mind and heart is so great as to cause even a cynic to suspect the action of the Holy Spirit when a genuine conversion from Satanism to God occurs. It is almost too much to hope that one could move from utter and complete rebellion and hostility against one's parents, family, community—and even God—to contrition, confession, and commitment; yet this can and does happen. "From darkness to light" describes the spiritual journey of many human beings, as the Book of Acts testifies, from Paul, to those Ephesians who burned their magic books and believed the Gospel.

The celebrated conversions of the past did not happen quickly or easily. Paul breathed threats and murder against the followers of Christ and was not content to persecute only in Jerusalem. While he moved persecution and hatred to the international scene, on the way to Damascus, the confrontation with Christ changed his life. Interestingly, the vision utterly confused Paul, and he needed a preacher to interpret what had happened to him.

We may partly explain the overthrowing of pagan idols and magical practices in Ephesus by the awe of the Ephesians, who saw in the miracles that followed Paul's missionary work a greater magic than the one they possessed. Undoubtedly, it took a lot of preaching and teaching to truly convert and Christianize even these willing ex-pagans.

Some Suggestions for the Concerned

To carry out the baptismal vow to "renounce the devil and all his works," to put away all the empty promises of the evil one, means we must each of us prepare ourselves as fully equipped Christian disciples. We must know our faith, the Scriptures, and our duty to proclaim the way of salvation in Christ to all, not just to those who welcome it or do not actively oppose our witnessing. Destructive occultists represent "hard cases" by which we can fairly test the reality of our commitment to proclaim the faith. Regardless of the complexities, the evasions, the resistance, or the shallow or even false conversions we meet in dealing with the hard cases of society (as in prison inmates, drug users, or occultists), the Christian must believe that only through replacement of the demonic influence by the spiritual, by faith in Christ, can the destructive occultist be freed from oppression and enter into salvation.

While we should never become tolerant of sin and idolatry, we need to remain open to people caught up in sin. Many times those fascinated by or oppressed by the occult feel shut out by Christians. If we close the church door to such persons, we have sinned by judging and condemning them. We must make ourselves available, keeping our minds and hearts open to all people, no matter how weird, strange, or frightening they may seem in human terms. Though we cannot force those involved in the occult to taste of God's mercy, we can offer it and leave the door open for them to come in at their own pace and time.

We must learn not to be afraid. Certainly we should recognize the dangers involved in destructive occultism and the personal danger that can come from interaction with some cultists of a criminal bent, yet we should also recognize that danger did not stop the missionaries of the early church or those modern missionaries who have died trying to evangelize native tribes in South America. Nominal faith, superficial Christianity, cannot match convinced occultists—or proponents of any other error. Often, when we swallow our distaste and our fear of the bizarre personalities involved in occultism, we find that faith takes over and gives us the courage to witness, to love, and to accept the sinner.

Oppose the teachings of hell with the teachings of love. Stress the ever-open arms of a loving God and the concerned heart and extended hand of a forgiving Savior. The threat of hell does not provide much motivation for those who have made a pact with it and are in league with Satan.

Accept those seeking a way out of their destructive lifestyle. Apologize to yourself for the language and dress of those steeped in alienation and self-loathing. Refrain from passing judgment in your actions as well as your words. Judgment belongs to God, who knows each heart and each person's history as persons do not. Speak in terms of accepting the Lord as a friend, rather than in terms of surrender. The destructive occultist who may be having second thoughts wishes to escape domination. Don't offer another form of slavery. Hold out the promise of Christian liberty, of God-given human freedom.

Patiently and gently deal with those entrapped in oppressive life-styles, whether it be alcohol or drug abuse, religious cults, or the destructive occult. Don't expect an emerging occultist to throw off all errors at once. Don't expect instantaneous, total acceptance of all you may say. Let your life and your behavior toward the person preach its own silent but effective sermon. Love the lost into the Body of Christ.

Upon significant change or an informed expression of the desire to accept Christ, accept that person without reservation and without making him or her an exhibit, a trophy to hold up before others in public meetings. Christ saves souls; He does not give us spiritual scalps to flaunt in public. When the Holy Spirit does his work through the damaged instruments of grace that we are, there is room for gratitude, not triumphalism.

Move on to assist the ex-occultist to become fully integrated into the church. Where necessary, provide physical care and a safe place, for underground cults may seek to retaliate against what they consider turncoats. Assist the newly converted to receive any medical attention and the proper level of psychological evaluation and counseling he may need. Since destructive occultism is so intimately tied up with substance abuse, you may need to find an alcohol or drug treatment program for the new convert. Do not avoid medical and secular psychological help when it seems warranted. Religious instruction and inspiration cannot substitute for some of the fine substance abuse programs and counseling services found in any large community.

Preach, teach, baptize, counsel, heal—use every resource available to assist the Satanist to a normal life. God has called us to peace and to the integration of all his scattered children into His peaceable kingdom.

Christ has died. Christ has risen. Christ has conquered sin, death, the power of the law, and the devil. Christ is the victor. Christ has beaten Satan down under our feet. When we see clearly, we see that God is on the throne. May he open our eyes, and may we help the eyes of many others to be opened also.

Notes

Chapter 1

1. *See* my books, *Religion in the Age of Aquarius* (Philadelphia: Westminster Press, 1971); *Throwing the Sticks* (Bristol, Ind.: Wyndham Hall, 1985); with Una McManus, *Not for a Million Dollars* (Nashville, Tenn.: Impact Books, 1980); and Una McManus, *Dealing With Destructive Cults* (Grand Rapids, Mich.: Zondervan Publishing Co., 1984).
2. David Breskin, "Kids in the Dark," *Rolling Stone* (November 22, 1984).
3. *CAN (Cult Awareness Network) News*, 5, no. 1 (January 1989), 1. *See also* "Teen Admits Killing, Cutting up Mother in Satanic Ritual," *The Orlando Sentinel* (March 18, 1989), 15.
4. Jeff Lilley, "Evil in the Land," *Moody Monthly*, 89, no. 7 (March, 1989), 14–16.
5. *Ibid.*
6. *Ibid.*, 8, as reported in *Sunday Oklahoman*.
7. "Scary Stuff in an Area High School," Moscow, Idaho, *Tribune* (February 9, 1989).
8. Jill Rauh, "Worship of Satan Leaving Its 'Mark' on Berrien County," *The Herald-Palladium* (April 8, 1989), 1.

9. Rex Springston, "Experts Say Tales Are Bunk," *Richmond News Leader* (April 6, 1989), 1.
10. *Ibid.*
11. Maury Terry, *The Ultimate Evil* (Garden City, N.Y.: A Dolphin book / Doubleday & Co., 1987). Lauren Stratford, *Satan's Underground* (Eugene, Ore.: Harvest House Publishers, 1988).

Chapter 2

1. John Charles Cooper, *The New Mentality* (Philadelphia: Westminster Press, 1969). Charles A. Reich, *The Greening of America* (New York: Random House, 1970).
2. Theodore Roszak, *The Making of a Counter Culture* (New York: Doubleday & Co., 1969).
3. I studied that brief theological fad in my books *The Roots of the Radical Theology* (Philadelphia: Westminster Press, 1967); and *Radical Christianity and Its Sources* (Philadelphia: Westminster Press, 1968).
4. Cooper, *Roots*, 13. *Italics added.*
5. Thomas J. J. Altizer, *Oriental Mysticism and Biblical Eschatology* (Philadelphia: Westminster Press, 1961); William Hamilton, *The New Essence of Christianity* (New York: Association Press, 1961).
6. Paul Tillich, *The Shaking of the Foundations* (New York: Charles Scribner's Sons, 1948). Dietrich Bonhoeffer, *No Rusty Swords* (New York: Harper & Row, 1965). John A. T. Robinson, *Honest to God* (Philadelphia: Westminster Press, 1963). Paul Van Buren, *The Secular Meaning of the Gospel* (New York: Macmillan Co., 1963). Gabriel Vahanian, *The Death of God* (New York: George Braziller, 1961). Martin Buber, *The Eclipse of God* (New York: Harper & Row/Harper Torch Books, 1957). Albert Camus, *The Plague*, trans. Stuart Gilbert (New York: Alfred A. Knopf, 1957). Jean-Paul Sartre, *No Exit* (New York: Vintage Books/Random House, 1955). Walker Percy, *The Moviegoer* (New York: Alfred A.

Knopf, 1961). John Updike, *Couples* (Greenwich, Conn.:
Fawcett Publications, 1969). John Gardner, *October Light*
(New York: Alfred A. Knopf, 1976).

7. Richard L. Rubenstein, *After Auschwitz* (Indianapolis: Bobbs-
Merrill Co., 1966). Kenneth Hamilton, *The System and the
Gospel* (New York: Macmillan Co., 1963). Langdon Gilkey,
Naming the Whirlwind (Indianapolis: Bobbs-Merrill Co.,
1969). Cooper, *Roots,* and Cooper, *Radical Christianity.*

8. John Charles Cooper, *The Roots of the Radical Theology* (Lan-
ham, Md.: University Press of America, 1988).

9. I chronicled these in *The New Mentality* and *Religion in the
Age of Aquarius* (Philadelphia: Westminster Press, 1971).

10. I made some attempt to document this in *The Turn Right*
(Philadelphia: Westminster Press, 1970).

11. George Gallup, Jr., and David Poling, *The Search for America's Faith* (Nashville, Tenn.: Abingdon Press, 1980), 17.

12. Cooper, *Aquarius,* 13ff.

13. Alvin Toffler, *Future Shock* (New York: Random House,
1970).

14. Cooper, *Throwing the Sticks,* 7–8.

15. *Ibid.,* 22.

16. Ralph Barton Perry, *Puritanism and Democracy* (New York:
1944).

17. Marshall McLuhan and Quentin Fiore, *The Media Is the Message* (New York: Bantam Books, 1967); *War and Peace in the
Global Village* (New York: Bantam Books, 1968).

Chapter 3

1. Rossell Hope Robbins, *The Encyclopedia of Witchcraft and Demonology* (New York: Crown Publishers, 1970), 371.

2. Stephen Vincent Benet, *The Devil and Daniel Webster* (New
York: Holt, Rinehart and Winston, 1965).

3. Christopher Marlowe, *Doctor Faustus* (New York: Signet
Classic/New American Library, 1969), vii–viii.

4. Robbins, *Encyclopedia*, 379.
5. Ronald Holmes, *Witchcraft in History* (Secaucus, N. J.: The Citadel Press, 1977), 16.
6. Robbins, *Encyclopedia*, 80–88, passim.
7. *Ibid.*
8. *Ibid.* 83.
9. *Ibid.*
10. *Ibid.*, 84.
11. Kurt Seligmann, *The History of Magic and the Occult* (New York: Harmony Books, 1975), 300–302.
12. *Ibid.*, 302.
13. *Malleus Maleficarum*, trans. Montague Summers (London: Hogarth Press, 1969), xiii.
14. Robbins, *Encyclopedia*, 51–52.
15. Blaise Pascal, "Misere de L'Homme Sans Dieu," *Pensées et Opuscules Philosophiques, Extraits* (Paris: Libraire Hachette, 1931), Part 2, 15ff.
16. M. Scott Peck, *People of the Lie* (New York: Simon & Schuster, 1983).
17. Aleister Crowley, *777*, second revision (privately printed by O.T.O., n.d.). Aleister Crowley, *The Book of the Law* (*Liber al val Legis*) (Pasadena, Calif.: Church of Thelema, 1926), 46 pages.
18. Crowley, *Book of the Law*.
19. *Ibid.*
20. *Ibid.*
21. *Ibid.*
22. Anton Szandor LaVey, *The Satanic Bible* (New York: Avon Books, 1969).
23. *Ibid.*, 23–24.
24. *Ibid.*, 24.
25. Anton Szandor LaVey, *The Satanic Rituals* (New York: Avon Books, 1972).

26. *Ibid.*, 11–12.
27. *Ibid.*, 12.
28. Mary Daly, *Beyond God the Father* (Boston: Beacon Press, 1973). Rosemary Radford Ruether, "Goddesses and Witches: Liberation and Counterculture Feminism," *The Christian Century* (September 10–17, 1980).
29. "Holy Baptism," *The Book of Common Prayer* (New York: The Church Hymnal Corporation/The Seabury Press, 1977), 302 ff.

Chapter 4

1. Michelle Smith and Lawrence Pazder, *Michelle Remembers* (New York: Pocket Books, 1987). On MPD *see:* Richard P. Kluft, M.D., "An Introduction to Multiple Personality Disorder," *Psychiatric Annals* 14 (1): 19–24, 1984; Cornelia B. Wilbur, M.D., "Multiple Personality and Child Abuse, An Overview," *Psychiatric Clinics of North America* (March, 1984), no. 1; Richard P. Kluft, M.D., "An Update on Multiple Personality Disorder," *Hospital and Community Psychiatry* (April, 1987), no. 4.
2. This material on Caribbean and African cults with similarities to Satanism results from my studies that were set in motion when United States Marshal Sam Gonzales asked me to give a "threat assessment" of an occult act directed toward a drug enforcement agent in Texas. This act was done by members of Constanzo's Matamoros drug smuggling and ritual murder cult (April, 1989). Books consulted included Walter Burkert et al., *Violent Origins* (Stanford, Calif.: Stanford University Press, 1987), and Victor Turner, *The Ritual Process* (Ithaca, N.Y.: Cornell University Press, 1977). The assessment is entitled "An Analysis of the Black Occultic Murders in Matamoros, Mexico," copyrighted by John Charles Cooper, Ph.D.

Chapter 5

1. *The Miami Herald* (February 10, 1989).
2. Carl R. Raschke, "Satanism and the Devolution of the New Religions," *SCP Newsletter* (Fall, 1985), No. 3, 26.
3. Hal Lindsey with C. C. Carlson, *Satan Is Alive and Well on Planet Earth* (Grand Rapids, Mich.: Zondervan Publishing House, 1972).
4. Vincent Bugliosi with Curt Gentry, *Helter Skelter* (New York: Bantam Books, 1975). *See also* Ed Sanders, *The Family* (New York: Avon Books, 1972).
5. Daniel Cohen, *The New Believers: Young Religion in America* (Oakland, Calif.: LC Publishing, 1975), 137.
6. Maury Terry, *The Ultimate Evil* (Garden City, N. Y.: A Dolphin Book / Doubleday & Co., 1987).

Chapter 6

1. Anton Szandor LaVey, *The Satanic Bible* (New York: Avon Books, 1969).
2. Anton Szandor LaVey, *The Satanic Rituals* (New York: Avon Books, 1972).
3. Maury Terry, *The Ultimate Evil* (Garden City, N. Y.: A Dolphin Book/Doubleday & Co., 1987). Terry reports many German Shepherds were slain ritualistically on the Croton Avenue Aqueduct path in Yonkers. (*See* photos between pages 154 and 155 and page 511. Terry discusses this area in chapter 9, "The Process," 158 ff.)

Chapter 7

1. *File 18 Newsletter* (July 21, 1986). Edited by Lt. Larry M. Jones, Boise Police Department, Boise, Idaho 83704.
2. *Ibid.*
3. *Ibid.*

4. Maury Terry, Chapter 9, "The Process," *The Ultimate Evil* (Garden City, N.Y.: A Dolphin Book/Doubleday & Co., 1987), 16, 172.

5. H. E. Barnes and N. K. Teeters, *New Horizons in Criminology*, 3rd ed. (Englewood Cliffs, N.J.: Prentice-Hall Publishers, 1960).

6. Michelle Smith and Lawrence Pazder, *Michelle Remembers* (New York: Pocket Books, 1987).

7. The child abuse in the Children of God, now called the Family of Love, is documented in John Charles Cooper with Una McManus, *Not for a Million Dollars* (Nashville, Tenn.: Impact Books, 1980).

8. John Charles Cooper and Una McManus, *Dealing With Destructive Cults* (Grand Rapids, Mich.: Zondervan Publishing House, 1984).

Chapter 8

1. Coroner Donald Butler, of Metcalfe County, Kentucky, gave a seminar on this occult crime to the international meeting of the Coroner's Association.

2. Oliver Johnson, *The Individual and the Universe* (New York: Holt Rinehart Winston, 1981), 176.

3. Saul Levine, *Radical Departures* (New York: Harcourt Brace Jovanovich, 1984).